HORROR
FILMS

HORROR FILMS

NIGEL ANDREWS

admiral

This book was devised and produced by Multimedia Publications (UK) Ltd

Editor: Richard Rosenfeld
Assistant Editor: Sydney Francis
Production: Karen Bromley
Design: Roger Kohn
Picture Research: David Sutherland

First published in the United Kingdom 1986 by Admiral Books an imprint owned jointly by WH Smith and Son Limited, Registered No 237811, England, trading as WHS Distributors, St John's House, East Street, Leicester LE1 6NE and Multimedia Publications (UK) Limited, Central House, 1 Ballards Lane, London N3 1UZ.

ISBN 1 85171 022 1

Typeset by Flowery Typesetters
Origination by Imago
Printed in Italy by Sagdos, Milan

Page 1 *Your vampire needs you. Christopher Lee points the finger in* ***Dracula AD 1972*** *(director Alan Gibson), one of his six outings as the Carpathian Count for Hammer Films.*

Pages 2-3 *Terror strikes small-town America. Masked menaces have been a hit with audiences ever since* ***The Texas Chainsaw Massacre*** *(1974) – this one is from* ***Halloween II*** *(director Rick Rosenthal, 1983).*

Pages 4-5 *How to rescue a child from hell-fire without really frying. American suburbia is in trouble again in* ***Poltergeist*** *(1982), directed by Tobe Hooper for producer Steven Spielberg, fresh from* ***E.T.*** *(1982).*

Endpapers *Stephen King's* ***Creepshow*** *(1982), written for director George A. Romero, featured this Yeti among its compendium of stories scripted and shot in a horror-comic style.*

CONTENTS

1

Ogres and Occupiers

To begin with a declaration – and one which in the age of the "video nasties" campaign and other attempts to clamp our screens is sorely needed. There is nothing meretricious, degrading or brutalizing about the best horror films. Nor even, if one looks at them with a searching eye and ignores the shrieks of today's self-appointed moral crusaders, about most of the *worst* horror films. The imagery of horror in the cinema can be as profound as poetry, as haunting as dreams, and as intense as the emotional need in audiences that it satisfies. And that need is for art – not just "high art" but also entertainment – to help us cope with the fear of death. Horror is the advance messenger of death, and by vicariously confronting him, trembling at him, but finally outfacing him, we can square up to both life and death with new spirit and courage.

Thus it needs to be insisted on that horror films are not for the morbid, they're for the life-lovers. They dangle ghoulies and ghosties before us for 90-odd minutes and then whisk them away to reveal – hey presto – we're still alive and kicking, the exit-doors are unchained, and no monster or demon blocks our path back to daylight.

Furthermore, watching horror films, like having nightmares, can have a cathartic benefit. We take all our hidden anxieties, throw them in the "launderette" of art or fantasy, spin them round and then hang them out to dry – so that we can look at them anew and find they're not really so grim and bloodstained after all. We can even wear them again, as we assuredly will, since nightmares do not destroy anxieties (not at first go, anyway); they merely help to objectify and clarify them. And we can wear them again in the knowledge that they need not cling to us unchanged for life, but can occasionally join other people's anxieties in the communal rinse. A fear shared is a fear reduced, and even perhaps finally exorcised.

Ogres and occupiers

Fear of death comes in two main shapes and sizes, and so do horror films. We can die, as we were created, by the Big Bang or Steady State. The Big Bang is the club over the head, the knife to the heart, or the gunshot through the brain. This is death the ogre, who crashes uninvited through the door or wall, lumbers a pace or two towards us and swats us into the next world.

The other death, the Steady State, is the slow decline by illness or disease. This is death the occupier: a parasite or succubus who deceives at first by his gentleness and suavity, but who ends by annexing our whole body.

No wonder the two great archetypes of horror films are Frankenstein's monster and Dracula: they represent the Big Bang and Steady State opposites of terror. Frankenstein's creature, that do-it-youself experiment which went horribly wrong, is an out-of-control ogre with thrown-off chains and pendulum walk who thump-foots towards us intending grievous bodily harm. We may die or we may live, but with this assailant there will certainly be no in-between.

Previous page *Blood and circuses. Two vampires make a meal of their latest victim in Hammer's* ***Vampire Circus*** *(director Robert Young, 1972).*

Above *Christopher Lee dons the grisly face-putty to play the cinema's most famous monster* ***The Curse of Frankenstein*** *(Terence Fisher, 1957).*

Right *Hollywood gave birth to its first* ***Dracula*** *in 1931. Bela Lugosi played the Count, here lit from below in best demonic tradition.*

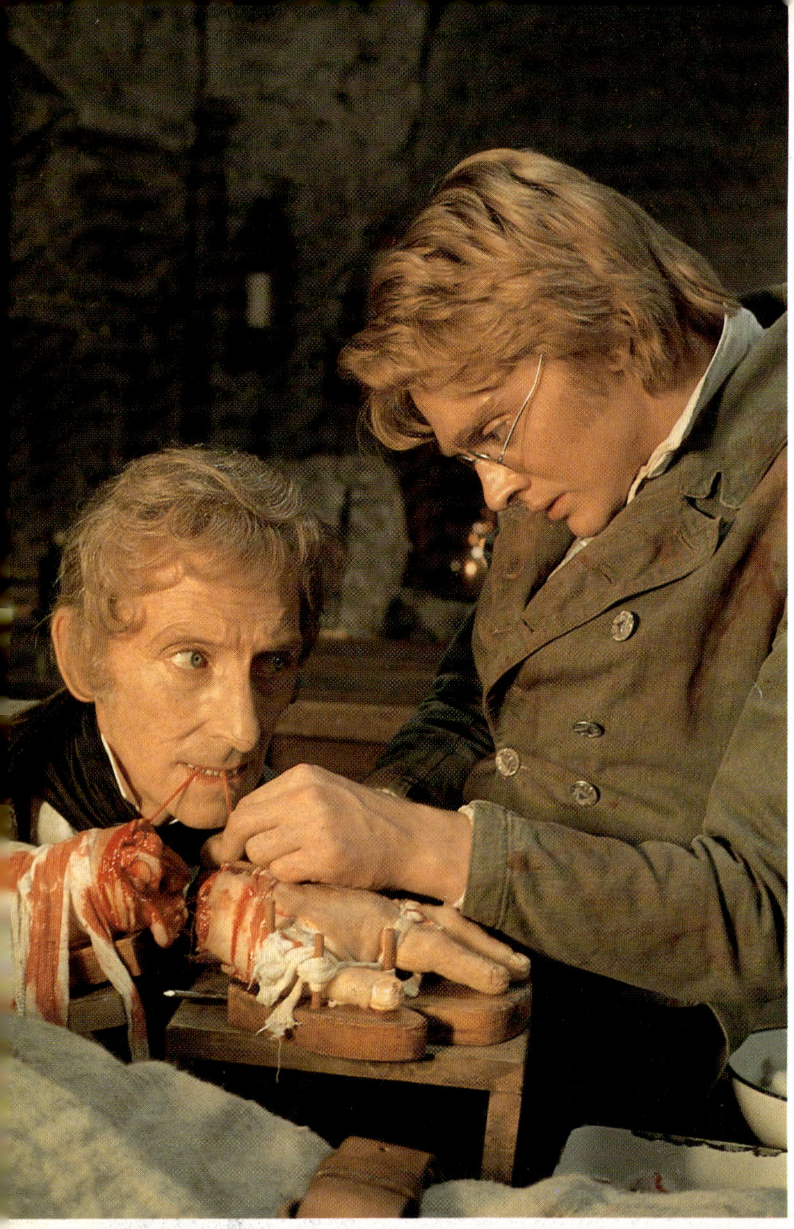

Dracula, by contrast, is a specialist in the in-between. He invariably begins by charming us, a Byronic host with a slightly upsetting pallor, but one whose conversation and dinner table hospitality are usually excellent. With the Count it is only later – when you rub that odd pair of seeming mosquito bites on your neck next morning – that you realize the process of Steady State destruction has begun.

Frankenstein's creature is the horror cinema's symbol for brusque and brutal death, in a plane crash, under a bus or head-first into a piece of factory machinery. Dracula is moviedom's emblem for slow, deceitful death, by wasting illness or the silent invasion of a spreading disease.

Machines of destiny

Frankenstein (let's call him that for convenience since we all know it's shorthand for Frankenstein's creature) leads a whole pack of ogres through the *danse macabre* of cinema history. And it's these we'll be looking at in Chapter 2. Although the assembly-kit monster born of Mary Shelley's novel was not the *first* of the cinema's horrific hulks – the eponymous ogre of Germany's 1914 **The Golem** probably claims that honor – he has been certainly the most influential. Scores of spin-offs from James Whale's original 1931 **Frankenstein** have dotted the decades since then. He has been

Left *Peter Cushing looks on as Shane Briant learns basic surgery in Hammer's sixth Frankenstein film,* ***Frankenstein and the Monster From Hell*** *(Terence Fisher, 1973).*

Right *The result of all this sawing and stitching can be seen on Dave Prowse (later to be* ***Star Wars****' Darth Vader), who plays the creature.*

Left *Posters from two of Hollywood's most effective forays into the spook world. Haunted houses featured in* ***The Uninvited*** *(Lewis Allen, 1944), and the Caribbean undead in* ***I Walked With A Zombie*** *(Jacques Tourneur, 1943).*

given a Bride (1935), he has met the Wolf Man (1943), he has been regurgitated at least six times by Hammer Films (1950s and 1960s), he has been processed in 3D by Andy Warhol (1973) and he has been given the accolade of meeting Abbott and Costello (1948).

But as well as fathering his own spin-offs, Frankenstein has been honorary President of the international movie ogres club. He influenced the style, patterned the expectations and set the pace (about two miles per hour, with lumbering gait) for a whole genealogy of ten-foot totems and bandaged Behemoths. **The Mummy** (1932) sped into production almost immediately after **Frankenstein**, giving Boris Karloff another chance to display rheumatic menace, and it too founded a family of sequels. **King Kong** (1933), **The Thing from Another World** (1951), **The Creature from the Black Lagoon** (1954), **Night of the Living Dead** (1968) and numerous zombie epics also bow to the monster's influence, and so does many a Hyde, Hunchback and Incredible Hulk.

Of course, the key to these brutes – or most of them – is that they are machines of destiny: blind, unknowing bogeymen who terrify us in the same way as a violent accident or an Act of God. You cannot ascribe

Left *Valerie Leon, dressed to awaken the dead, looks on apprehensively to see if she has had that effect in* ***Blood From the Mummy's Tomb*** *(Hammer Films 1971, directors Seth Holt and Michael Carreras).*

Below *No horror icon, however powerful, was proof against a visit from Abbott and Costello. Here the comedy duo raised their hats to one such in* ***Abbott and Costello Meet the Mummy*** *(1955).*

Above *A skeleton-masked Lon Chaney – he looks even more hideous when he takes it off – terrifies the opera buffs in* ***The Phantom of the Opera*** *(1925). This is the best of four versions of the film.*

Above *If the soprano can't bring the house down, Claude Rains will.* ***The Phantom of the Opera*** *strikes again, in Universal's 1943 version directed by Arthur Lubin.*

Left *Brian De Palma's* ***Phantom of the Paradise*** *(1974) played a rock musical variation on the same theme, with strong injections of parody. Paul Williams starred and wrote the music.*

evil to them as you can to the vampire (with his scheming suavity and intelligence) because they are automata of Fate. They do not scheme or plan, they merely and horribly function. And what faint self-awareness some of them *do* have – notably King Kong and Frankenstein himself – is so low-burning that it inspires pity rather than condemnation. They are the horrors of the world represented as blind, dumb, implacable agents; programmed (if at all) only by some unseen and unseeable hand of destiny.

Evil by intent

The Dracula family, by contrast, and its relatives both close and distant, are keenly intelligent and keenly sentient. Theirs is the horror of *conscious* evil-doing; and perhaps also its pathos. Where the Frankenstein clan with a brute's instinct are ogres, attacking innocent human life from outside, the Draculas are occupiers, attacking from the inside. They scheme, they flatter, they cajole, they deceive, they infiltrate. Like a fatal illness, they will offer moments of hope or remission (the banquet in the Gothic dining-hall, the cultured conversation, the book thoughtfully left at the bedside). But once they have taken poisonous root inside the body, they are as sure and merciless as the more frontal fatality of the monster.

Like Frankenstein, Dracula was born into the worldwide movie consciousness in 1931 (although F. W. Murnau's 1922 **Nosferatu**, made in Germany, borrowed the character, if not the name, from Bram Stoker's original vampire novel). Having once sunk his teeth into his first victim – and his first movie audience – the Transylvanian blood-taster never looked back. Like Frankenstein, he sired a whole family of sequels, and though fashions changed *vis-à-vis* how the Count should *look* – from portly, sepulchral Bela Lugosi to poker-gaunt Christopher Lee – there was never any doubt that he was mannerly, menacing, impeccably dressed and insatiably fond of the crimson fluids.

The modest flood of Dracula films in the 1930s and 1940s – **Dracula's Daughter** (1936), **Return of the Vampire** (1944), **House of Dracula** (1945) and several more, including the inevitable meeting with Abbott and Costello (though this, ironically, was within the 1948 **Abbott and Costello Meet Frankenstein**) – were but a prelude to the dams bursting in the late 1950s. After Hammer's first go at floating the vampire Count in 1958, when millions of moviegoers goggled at Christopher Lee turning into ashes at the climax (it's good for the carpet, commented somebody at the Press screening), the patrician parasite returned again and again to ring Hammer's cash register: notably in **Dracula, Prince of Darkness** (1966), **Dracula Has

Above *Another bad day at the passport photo booth? No, just one of Hammer's* ***Twins of Evil*** *(John Hough, 1971), in which witchcraft and vampirism are picturesquely mixed.*

Left *A moment of impalement from Hammer's* ***Vampire Circus*** *(1972): one of its more desperate attempts to keep a sideshow vampire industry going without Christopher Lee.*

Below *Horror in glorious Eastman Colour. Hammer's first* ***Dracula*** *(Terence Fisher, 1958) set the trend for six more helpings of gore and Grand Guignol.*

Risen From the Grave (1968) and **Taste the Blood of Dracula** (1970).

The world soon caught wind, and Carpathia's leading export was hotfooting it to Hollywood again, sometimes for serious purposes, sometimes for spoof (as with George Hamilton's **Love at First Bite**, 1979) and sometimes in between. He was immortalized by Andy Warhol (**Blood for Dracula**, 1973), he was recognizable in all but name in **Count Yorga, Vampire** (1970) and he even seized his old nomenclature – plus the bat ears, rat teeth and two-inch finger-nails off his first German impersonator Max Schreck – in Werner Herzog's remake, **Nosferatu the Vampyre** (1979).

But like Frankenstein, Dracula is as interesting for the indirectly related movies he inspired as for the literal, and often literal-minded, spin-offs. The figure of the parasite or succubus – those creatures who lead with their lips or teeth, who seduce before they slay, who soothe and purr you into submission – shimmers into prominence in films like **Cat People** (1942 and 1982), **The Leopard Man** (1943), **The Black Cat** (1934) and even the title creatures who switch from "Ooh aah" cuteness to lethal predatoriness in **Gremlins** (1984).

Meanwhile, the whole theme of "possession" in horror movies and thrillers is vampire-related, and so is the whole motif of evil by contagion. In Chapter 3 we'll be looking at these themes and these horror figures – the occupiers as opposed to the ogres – and considering the different kind of frisson and menace they offer.

In Chapter 4, winging right into the present, 1980s horror movies come into view; and they offer a different kettle of plasma from either the Dracula group or the Frankenstein. The bloodsucking Count has vanished almost completely from today's Grand Guignol scene – except as raw material for spoofs – and poor Frankenstein has never really recovered (though the day may yet come) from the twin onslaught of television's **The Munsters** and cinema's **Young Frankenstein** (1974). So while Dracula turns into a vaudeville turn, busy swishing his cape, baring his fangs and extracting every last joke about blood or

Below *Love at First Bite (1978) led the way in a wave of vampire spoofs in the late 1970s. George Hamilton assesses the neck of Susan Saint James, a model whose face he saw on a magazine cover. She becomes a vampire, and they fly off, hand in hand.*

Right *One of the* ***Friday the 13th*** *(1980) saga's many unhappy returns. The promising mayhem of the first movie petered out in endless action-replay sequels. This is from* ***Part 2*** *(1981).*

Below *A young man pauses to turn into something savage and hairy. Transformation time in* ***Legend of the Werewolf*** *(1975).*

Left *A comely victim succumbs to devil worship in Hammer's* ***Twins of Evil*** *(1971); not their first, nor their last, attempt to combine the spine-chilling with the sexy.*

Above *Someone isn't using vampire repellent... A moment of terror from* ***Vampyres*** *(1975).*

dentistry, and Frankenstein is reduced to singing "Puttin' on the Ritz" for Mel Brooks, in what direction are today's horror films heading?

Visible violence

One direction is towards a new realism – or a new visceralism. The graphic depiction of horror and violence in films like **The Texas Chainsaw Massacre** (1974) paved the way for the present decade in which the motto seems often to be: violence must not only be done, it must be *seen* to be done. Even the once shocking shower scene in Hitchcock's **Psycho** (1960) now seems a masterpiece in artful impressionism – a flurry of cuts in the editing-room rather than a flurry of cuts on Janet Leigh's body – compared to the films of David Cronenberg (**Rabid, Scanners, Videodrome**) or Tobe Hooper (**The Texas Chainsaw Massacre, Death Trap, The Funhouse**). And then of course there are the "video nasties": the **Driller Killer, SS Experiment Camps, Zombie Flesh-Eaters** and the rest of that company.

Have myth and fantasy retreated completely before this surge of queasy realism? No. One feature of the 1980s has been the return of the werewolf: that weird changeling creature who comes over all funny, not to mention all furry, at full moon. Like an understudy awaiting his big night, the werewolf has charged onto the empty stage vacated by Frankenstein and Count D in the 1980s and has howled, growled, gored, mauled and metamorphosed away to his heart's content. **An American Werewolf in London, Wolfen, The Howling** and **The Company of Wolves** are but four examples of moviedom's gleeful determination to loop the lupine in this decade.

What these changes in horror fashion all mean, and why the two grand old archetypes have been elbowed out of the way, for the time being, in favor of new-minted monsters and demons (as in **Alien, Possession, The Thing, Gremlins**) and also in favor of an abattoir line in gory special effects, is something we'll discover as we go along.

Fashions of fright

But one thing is certain, and should be lit up in blazing neon from the beginning. The cinema of horror has never stood still, any more than has the cinema of sci-fi or the cinema of Westerns. Times change and so do the things people want to scream at.

You have only to look at 1959's **Plan 9 from Outer Space** or 1963's **Attack of the Mushroom People** to wonder how anyone could *ever* have screamed at them, except with laughter. And even the opposition I've suggested between the Dracula school and the Frankenstein school of horror film should not be taken too literally. They are merely opposite ends of a spectrum containing all shades of Gothic menace and mythic symbolism in between.

There are also cross-overs between the two schools. The most interesting exchange student is perhaps the "zombie". He spends half of each term at the Frankenstein Seminary for Young Monsters, where he learns to walk with a swaying clockwork motion, to stare ahead with unblinking eyes and to knock over absolutely anything (or anyone) standing in his way. Then he nips over to the Dracula School for the Incurably Undead, where he learns how to look extremely pale and how to frighten the life out of anyone trying to monkey with his immortality (though, like the vampire, he doesn't actually *enjoy* his immortality too much).

There were also, of course, the long years of cinematic horror – and *vintage* cinematic horror, at that – before Dracula and Frankenstein were even a gleam in Universal Studios' eye. But even here, especially in the most famous hothouse of silent horror artistry, 1920s Germany, the world of movie terror was divided prophetically between the ogres and the occupiers. Leading the ogres' team into battle was the Golem, actor-director Paul Wegener's magnificent lurching

Right *Lon Chaney, with a rictus grin, helps his daughter find her way in* ***London After Midnight*** *(1927). This tale of modern-dress vampirism was written and directed by Tod Browning.*

Below *"It's my baby and I'll scream if I want to." Samantha Eggar clutches something alive and unpleasant in* ***The Brood*** *(David Cronenberg, 1979).*

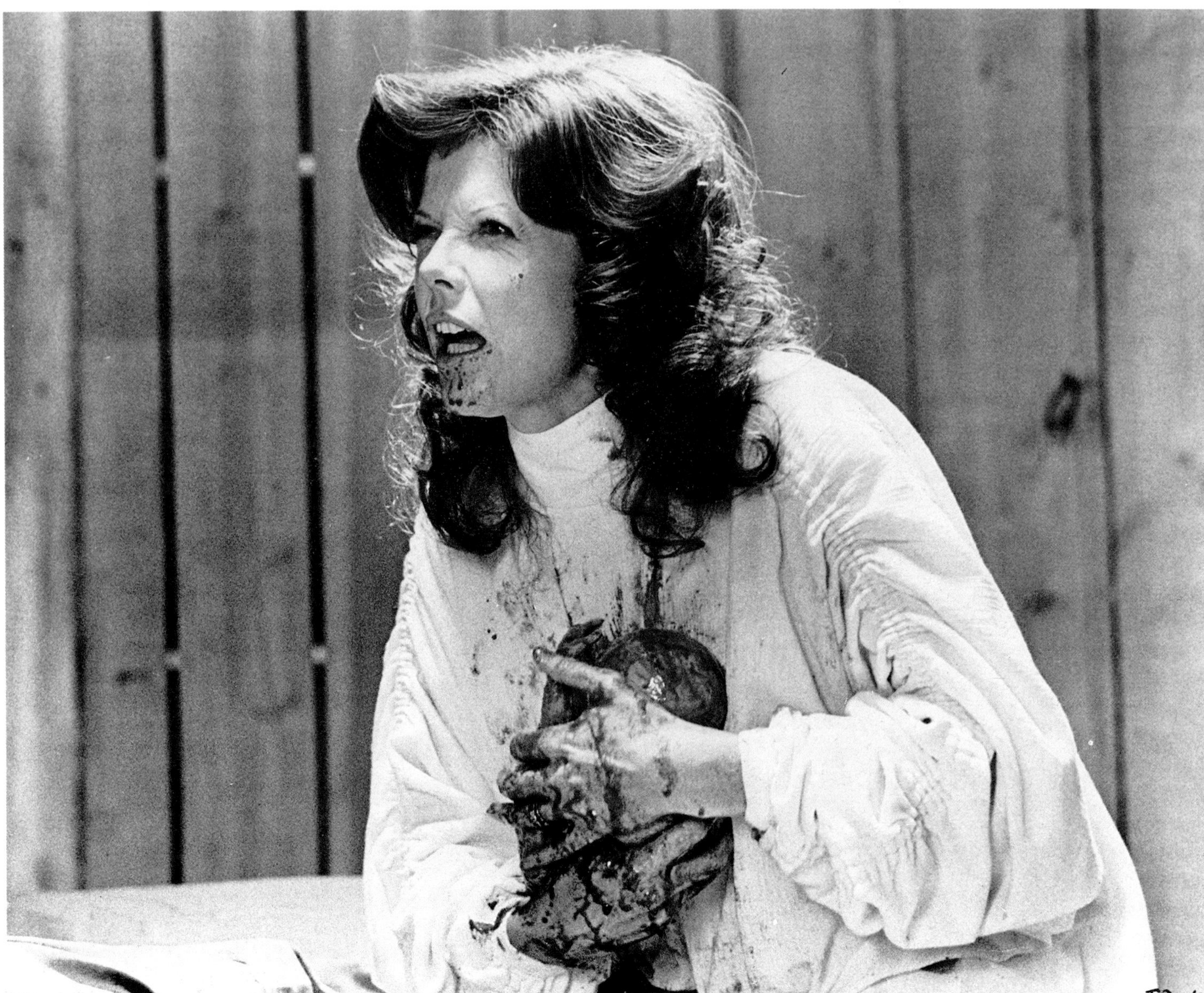

totem – a clay statue come to life – in the 1914 film of that name (and an avowed influence on the later director of **Frankenstein**, James Whale). Leading the occupiers' eleven was undoubtedly Dr Caligari, suavely evil manipulator and Machiavelli, controlling the soul of his murderous sleepwalking "patient", Cesare, in **The Cabinet of Dr Caligari** (1919). (There was also Drac himself popping up, of course, under the sobriquet of Nosferatu in the 1922 German film.)

Poles apart

Throughout the history of movie horror these poles of evil have existed: the brutal and the beguiling, the lumbering monster and the suave parasite, the ogre and the occupier. The ogre works by blind instinct, a walking juggernaut put into forward gear by an unseen hand. His trail of trampling destruction is all the more frightening for being involuntary and therefore unreasoned. You can't stop Frankenstein or the Mummy or King Kong in mid-march and try and sweet-reason them out of their murderous progress. They'll simply pound on towards you, and Heaven help you if you're still in their way when they reach you.

The occupier, by contrast, will listen sweetly to every guest who enters his castle, every potential victim who enters his lair. He's the spider at the heart of a web. He blandishes and beguiles, he's the perfect host. And when he pounces it's not with brute violence but with a subtle poison or contagion that paralyzes the will. He prefers to create live – or half live – slaves and disciples to dead victims.

But it's with the Frankenstein family – the ogres – that we begin …

Below *One of Hollywood's more eccentric monsters graced this 1958 sci-fi fantasy* ***The Fly****. More fi than sci, but it returned for a sequel the following year.*

2

The Monster Club

In sixteenth-century Prague a Rabbi makes a statue of clay and brings it to life. Grim, huge, grey, barrel-chested – with only his white and mobile eyes firing a warning salvo of violence – he serves his master docilely for a time. And then, spurred by unrequited love for the Rabbi's daughter (who not surprisingly greets his overtures with horror), he goes on the rampage through the twisting, tortuous, beetling streets until finally he is destroyed by a fall from a high tower.

This is the Golem, title monster of Paul Wegener and Henrik Galeen's 1914 film: the finest early flower of German Expressionism and the first authentic horror classic. **The Golem** also laid out the ground rules for almost every "ogre movie" the cinema would produce in the next seventy years. The initially innocent monster, awakened by life and passion, reaches the screen again in **Frankenstein** and **King Kong.** The ogre as Nemesis, visiting violence on those who rouse him from his timeless slumber, returns a further time in the myriad Mummy films that whirred into action in the 1930s and after. And even the pathos that makes our hearts go out to King Kong or Frankenstein (or, on a good day, to Godzilla or Gorgo) is present in the Golem's lovelorn and inarticulate clumsiness.

Previous page *Things that go squelch in the night... A monster embraces his terrified victim in* ***Mutations*** *(1973).*

Man-made monsters

Also crucial to many of these films, beginning with **The Golem**, is the master-slave or inventor-robot relationship. Whereas a nature-born monster of the jungle or the deep seas, like Kong or Godzilla or Gorgo, does not require a human creator, a robot or automaton most certainly does. So films like **The Golem, Metropolis** (1926), **Frankenstein** (1931) and **The Bride of Frankenstein** (1935) evolve into parables of human presumption, with man playing God and turning base clay or metal into living creatures shaped in his own image. The punishment for this arrogance is that the creatures then turn on their makers, in anger at their own ugliness or ill-finished "humanity", and hound, harry or destroy them.

Indeed, there are few monster movies of *any* kind in which the ogre's rampagings are not linked to some fable of human presumption, of man's attempts to mold, tame or subjugate Nature. King Kong himself goes berserk when he's put in chains and forced to become an outsize fairground freak in New York.

Below *The title hero of Germany's* ***The Golem*** *(Paul Wegener, 1914) was a clay statue come to life, based on an old Jewish myth of an unhappy monster without a soul, whose love for a beautiful girl is spurned. He was the cinema's first anticipation of Frankenstein.*

Left *The strong arm of the law meets the dismembered arm of one of the creature's victims in* ***Son of Frankenstein*** *(1939). An unworthy sequel, but Karloff was still in fine form as the monster.*

Below *Kong versus the USAF in the greatest monster film of its time – or all time? –* ***King Kong.*** *Year, 1932. Setting, top of the Empire State Building, New York.*

This idea of the ogre as Nemesis is startlingly pervasive in Germany's great period of silent horror cinema, from **The Golem** in 1914 to **Metropolis** in 1926. In Robert Wiene's **The Cabinet of Dr Caligari** (1919) the "ogre" is not a literal monster or automaton, but in the shape of the sleepwalker Cesare (Conrad Veidt) he has exactly the same murderous and mechanistic inexorability. And his evil, overweening master Dr Caligari (Werner Krauss) ends by being exposed and brought to justice (though in the cunning framing device later added by Wiene, the whole film, it's suggested, is a tale told by an "idiot" in Dr Caligari's asylum).

If the Golem is the prototype for Frankenstein, Cesare in **Caligari** is the prototype for succeeding generations of movie zombies: those sleepless sleepwalkers raised from the dead, usually at the bidding of an evil master eager for a mute and pliant labor force to execute his errands.

More early classics

Three other German silent films are vital to our ogre studies. In Paul Leni's **Waxworks** (1924) – the German title is **Das Wachsfigurenkabinett**, deliberately invoking memories of an earlier "Cabinet" – three tales are told, inspired by three figures in a wax museum: Haroun-al-Raschid, Ivan the Terrible, and Jack the Ripper. The tone gets darker as the film proceeds, from the knockabout oriental antics of Emil Jannings as Raschid via the mist-laden menace of Ivan's Russia (with Conrad Veidt as the Czar) to the horrific, shadow-stricken scamperings of the Ripper (Werner Krauss) through a twisted, writhing, studio-built London. Just as the

Below *Cesare the murdering somnambulist (Conrad Veidt) seizes a lady victim in the classic German horror film* ***The Cabinet of Dr Caligari*** *(Robert Wiene, 1919).*

Above *Raymond Massey has a difference of opinion with Boris Karloff (bearded) in* ***The Old Dark House*** *(James Whale, 1932), one of the earliest "spoof" horror films.*
Left *Grisly goings-on in the silent German masterpiece* ***Waxworks*** *(1924), Paul Leni's trip through the horrors of history from Haroun-al-Raschid to Jack the Ripper.*
Overleaf ***Frankenstein*** *(1931) – the film that launched a hundred sequels; and the career of a hitherto unknown British actor William Pratt, better known as Boris Karloff.*

CARL LAEMMLE presents
FRANKENSTEIN
THE MAN WHO
MADE A MONSTER
with
COLIN CLIVE, MAE CLARKE,
JOHN BOLES, BORIS KARLOFF,
DWIGHT FRYE, EDW. VAN SLOAN & FREDERIC KERR
Based upon the
Mary Wollstonecraft Shelley Story
Adapted by John L. Balderston
from the play by Peggy Webling
DIRECTED BY
JAMES WHALE
A UNIVERSAL PICTURE
PRODUCED BY
CARL LAEMMLE, JR.

UNIVERSAL PRESENTA
FRANKENSTEIN
CON
COLIN CLIVE
MAE CLARKE
JOHN BOLES
BORIS KARLOFF
BASADA EN LA HISTORIA de MARY WOLLSTONE CROFT SHELLEY
DIRIGIDA POR JAMES WHALE

Golem came to sinister life from brute clay, these three tyrants and terrorizers are woken for us from inanimate wax; and in the process they founded yet another favorite horror genre, the wax museum chiller.

Equally influential on horror history was Robert Wiene's 1924 **The Hands of Orlac**. This has a new twist on the master-slave, owner-ogre relationship, for they become one and the same person. The murderer's hands grafted onto musician Conrad Veidt (he lost his own in a train crash) guide him horribly and helplessly into a series of killings. Here we see German cinema forerunning not only the "dismembered hand" school of shockers to come – those films in which grafted or truncated mitts run around with a life of their own trying to encourage evil deeds (**The Beast with Five Fingers**, 1947; **Hands of the Ripper**, 1971; **The Hand**, 1982) – but also the split-personality spine-chiller *à la* **Dr Jekyll and Mr Hyde** (1920, 1932 and 1941).

Fritz Lang's **Metropolis** (1926) is not a horror film in the true sense, but in the sixty years since it was made scarcely any horror film with a sci-fi tinge hasn't been influenced by it. Here is the ultimate mad scientist (Rudolph Klein-Rogge with 100-watt eyes and vertical-take-off hair) beavering away in the ultimate laboratory (all glowing tubes and hissing retorts) to create the ultimate robot. Sorry, robot*ess*: for there's none of your male chauvinism in this city of the future, and the automaton of destiny comes in the comely guise of Brigitte Helm. And the brilliant irony of **Metropolis** is that the story's true ogre – its figure of monstrous, insatiable brutality – is not Helm's metal-plated siren at all but the monster incarnated in the society itself: the Moloch god who materializes out of the factory machinery to gobble up the weary, shuffling processions of victim-workers.

Metropolis views human "progress" – in science, technology, industry and architecture – with mixed wonder and horror. And, throughout movie history, the ogre has been a symbol for the second of those responses: man's overweening tinkerings with Nature and his attempts to usurp God's role in creating life are punished with the boomerang vengeance or violence of his own creations. They shake off their chains, straps or bandages and come galumphing towards him, maddened monsters with metronome walks. And he will either run for his life or end up as a nasty accident on the laboratory floor.

Hollywood's horror boom

With **Frankenstein** in 1931 nearly all these threads and themes come together. Frankenstein's monster is the ogre as Nemesis; he's the ogre as nightmare incarnation of Progress; and he's the ogre as both symbol and punishment of his master's arrogance and of man's attempt to usurp God's prerogative as Creator. But he's also (like the Golem) an innocent with the dim stirrings of human feeling and (like Cesare in **Caligari**) a guiltless creature-of-instinct driven to Evil by imperatives beyond his understanding.

Boris Karloff strode the role like a Colossus with that pale and ghastly head like an upturned bucket rudely stamped with features, those plug-in electrodes in the neck (at least Dracula would get a nasty shock if he tried a bite), that stomping heavy-footed walk (as if he had a sledgehammer in each boot) and that voice pitiably grunting and straining as if weighed down with all the sorrows of the world.

Whale's direction, as befits the power of Mary Shelley's story, is like a Greek tragedy gone Gothic. And the scene of the monster's creation, that outrage against the heavens, almost reaches Heaven itself as the roof of Frankenstein's lab opens to the stormy midnight skies and God's own lightning-bolts are borrowed for the last surge of electricity.

Above *Wolfmen have stalked the horror cinema for years since* ***The Werewolf of London*** *(1935). This is an early contender in the lycanthropy stakes,* ***The Wolf Man*** *(1941).*

Left *Boris Karloff getting close on 4000 years of beauty sleep in **The Mummy** (Karl Freund, 1932), first of the Hollywood plunderings in Ancient Egypt.*

Above *Andrea King has a nasty turn in **The Beast With Five Fingers** (1947). Actually it is four fingers and a thumb, but who's counting? Robert Florey directed.*

No wonder, with **Frankenstein**'s success, that Hollywood promptly went monster-mad. The next year, 1932, saw **The Mummy** crashing into being, with Karloff once more ogre-ing into action as a 4000-year-old Egyptian corpse. The film, though unremarkable, went on to spawn almost as many spin-offs as **Frankenstein** itself, such was its success.

In the same year there were Tod Browning's **Freaks**, depicting the nastier side of circus life, James Whale's horror comedy **The Old Dark House** (again with Karloff, who must have been on a conveyor belt from one Gothic film set to the next), Michael Curtiz' **Mystery of the Wax Museum** (Lionel Atwill as the mutilated museum-owner whose face launches a thousand shrieks) and Charles Laughton presiding over a tropical menagerie of mutants and the mutilated in **The**

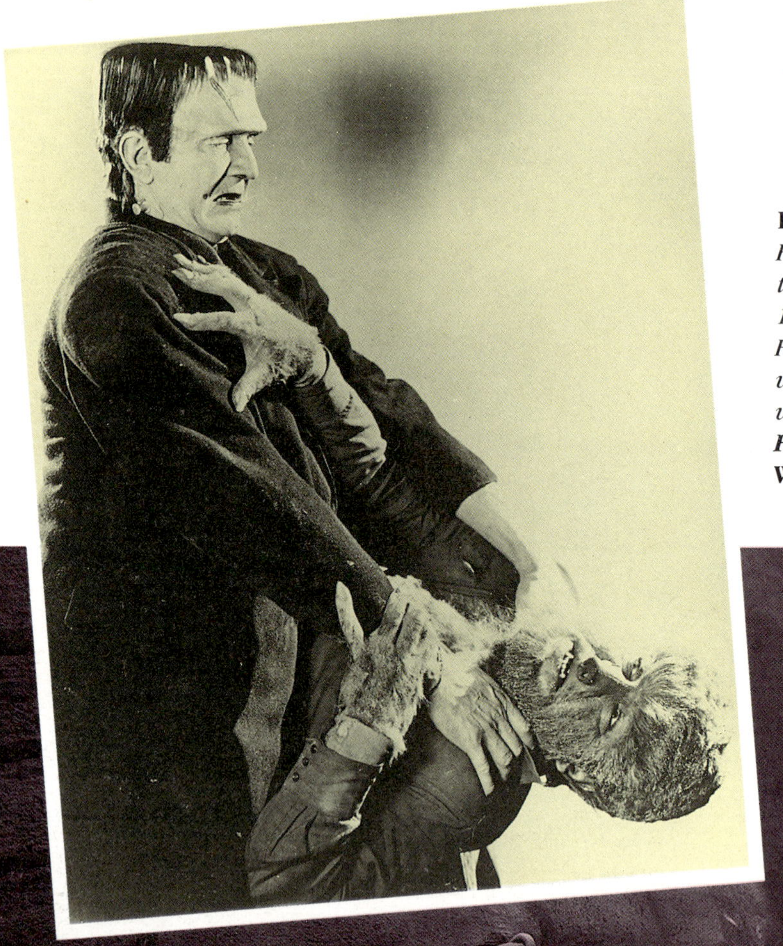

Left *There was no stopping Frankenstein as he romped through sequels in the 1930s and early 1940s. Here he meets a fellow ogre who is clearly getting the worst of things in* ***Frankenstein Meets the Wolf Man*** *(1943).*

Below *He declines the offer of a light from a friendly gaoler in the original* ***Frankenstein*** *(1931).*

Mummy movies through the ages. **Right** *Boris Karloff glowering under a fez as "Imhotep" in* ***The Mummy*** *(1931).* **Above** *Christopher Lee dons the bandages and fixed stare to attack Peter Cushing in Hammer's first go at the genre,* ***The Mummy*** *(Terence Fisher, 1959).*

Island of Lost Souls, based on H.G. Wells' book *The Island of Dr Moreau.*

Prehistoric plunge

And in 1933 came **King Kong**. Kong starts off by being the largest and most menacing ogre in film history and by the end of the movie has become the most perversely lovable. How can you hate a monster whose chief crime is his *amour fou* for the heroine, played with shredded dresses and an astounding repertoire of screams by Fay Wray? The physical logistics of this relationship, of course, even if Miss Wray *had* said yes to Kong, defy speculation. Camels going through the

Left *"I've heard of a skeleton staff, but this is ridiculous!" Phyllis Kirk is troubled by her friend's undernourished look in* ***House of Wax*** *(1935).*

Below *Two menacing mutants confront slinky-clad Kathleen Burke in* ***Island of Lost Souls*** *(1932), Hollywood's version of H. G. Wells'* The Island of Dr Moreau.

Above *The most lovable monster of them all makes overtures to the most memorable damsel-in-distress. Kong and Fay Wray together in* ***King Kong*** *(Merian Cooper and Ernest Schoedsack, 1933).*

Right *"Put me down, you male chauvinist ape!" cried Jessica Lange in this 1976 remake of* ***King Kong*** *(John Guillermin). The original was less smart with the one-liners, but far superior in fantasy, excitement and thrills.*

eyes of needles are simple by comparison. But when has plausibility ever been at a premium in Hollywood?

The fascination of **King Kong** is that it's a plunge into prehistory. The uncharted island where Kong lives is a time-warped playground for pterodactyls, dinosaurs and their ilk, and this "lost world" becomes an atavistic admonishment to twentieth-century man: that in climbing towards his skyscraping future and his hi-tech heavens he'd better not forget the savage depths from which he came. Once again the "ogre" – if one dare insult Kong by such a name – is a Nemesis figure sent out to bash some moral or metaphysical sense into hubristic man.

The early 1930s was an astounding period for the horror film. Was the spate of shockers and chillers and monster movies a product of the Depression? Or a foreboding of the rise of Hitler? Or a coincidence? Or a knock-on response to the Gothic yarns screaming their way over from Germany?

What's certain is that all the main themes and archetypes for horror cinema to come were mapped out in these years: Dracula, Frankenstein, Jekyll and Hyde (not the first feature-length version – that was a dull, stagebound movie with John Barrymore in 1920 – but the second and best with Fredric March in 1932), wax museum, mummy, zombie (**White Zombie**, 1932) and even that most self-effacing of macabre heroes, **The Invisible Man** (1933).

Sequelitis

After this short and heady heyday, the horror film – especially the ogre film – went into a long period of stagnation until the end of the 1940s. Audiences must have felt stuck in some recurring nightmare as sequel after sequel – almost invariably inferior to its original – attempted to squeeze more milk from the recalcitrant udders. **Son of Kong** (1933), **Son of Frankenstein** (1939), **Dracula's Daughter** (1936), **The Invisible Man Returns** (1940), **The Invisible Woman** (!) (1941), **The Ghost of Frankenstein** (1942), **Son of Dracula** (1943), **Frankenstein Meets the Wolf Man** (1943)… Who knows? If war hadn't intervened we might have had **Nosferatu's Niece, Frankenstein's Second Cousin Twice Removed, Dracula's Dentist** and a host more intriguing variations. (Even some of the actors were follow-ons: Lon Chaney Jr being a particularly dire sequel to Lon Chaney Sr.)

The only light in the darkness of these years was Val Lewton, whose work as producer of some of the most eerie, oblique, poetic horror films in Hollywood history – **Cat People** (1942), **The Leopard Man** (1943), **The Seventh Victim** (1943) – will be discussed in the next chapter, where more subtle terror is our subject.

Below *Boris Karloff's Creature getting to know Elsa Lanchester as his intended in* ***The Bride of Frankenstein*** *(James Whale, 1935). Made with tongue partly in cheek, but full of Gothic panache.*

Right ***The Creature From the Black Lagoon*** *(1954) closes in for the kill. Julia Adams screams. Jack Arnold directed. The film made a fortune.*

Atomic monsters

It was in the 1950s that the ogre rose again, casting off the chains of derivation and swelling anew with the breath of science fiction. Suddenly things were charging at us from Outer Space, or burbling up from the ocean-bed after being disturbed by atomic tests. No longer were monsters and ogres required to have some identifiable zoological pedigree: they didn't have to be variations on wolves or cats or apes or leopards or bats, or even robots. They could just be "things". For this was the post-nuclear age and we'd all heard of mutation.

Sometimes ambition out-ran budget or imagination, or both. **The Creature From the Black Lagoon** (1954), covered from head to toe in scaly black rubber, looks merely like a frogman in a mysteriously rococo wetsuit. Far better is **The Beast From 20,000 Fathoms** (1953), a prehistoric lizard as big as a department store who goes on the rampage in New York, drawn by the prospect of limitless destruction, an offer few monsters can refuse: least of all the sci-fi ogres is Japan's **Godzilla** (1955), a Pacific-dwelling and hitherto pacific dragon who when disturbed by (yes) atomic tests insists on a day excursion to Tokyo in order to raze it to the ground.

Right *New York ravaged by runaway back-projection. Can the cops cope? The ogre in the background is* ***The Beast From 20,000 Fathoms*** *(Eugene Lourie, 1953).*

Left *Another Hollywood sci-fly movie. This was* ***The Return of the Fly*** *(1959), in which the buzzing pest once more made a nuisance of himself to Vincent Price and others. Good special effects, terrible script.*

Right above *Beware of strange creatures in highly-styled scuba suits. This 1954 romp,* ***The Creature From the Black Lagoon,*** *begat a whole series of stuntman-in-monster's-clothing movies. It was one of the best, especially in original 3D.*

Right below *Japan's* ***Gojira – Godzilla*** *to Western audiences – growled onto our screens in 1955 (director Inoshiro Honda). He flattened Tokyo, broke box-office records and spawned a series of sequels.*

CREATURE
FROM THE
BLACK LAGOON
starring
RICHARD CARLSON · JULIA ADAMS

It's Alive!
GODZILLA
KING OF THE MONSTERS!
RAYMOND BURR
Directed by TERRY MORSE & I. HONDA
A TRANS WORLD RELEASE
COPYRIGHT 1956 GODZILLA RELEASING COMPANY COUNTRY OF ORIGIN U.S.A.
Property of National Screen Service Corp. Licensed for display only in connection with the exhibition of this picture at your theatre. Must be returned immediately thereafter.
56 214

Left *Human screams rend the darkness as the impassive "thing" looks on. Fantasy, sci-fi and horror combine in* ***Tower of Evil,*** *(1974). Gary Hamilton is the screamer.*

Right *Quake in your boots, or giggle into your handkerchief, according to taste. Director Jacques Tourneur was not amused when this Halloween ogre was inserted by the studio into his subtle supernatural thriller* ***Night of the Demon*** *(1957).*

Let us not forget in passing the giant ants of **Them!** (1954), the giant octopus of **It Came From Beneath the Sea** (1955), the giant spider of **Tarantula** (1955), and the giant monster of **Behemoth the Sea Monster** (1959), rounding off the decade.

Hammer horrors

Meanwhile Frankenstein was not dead but sleeping. Hammer Films roused him from inertia in 1957 with their first bash at dramatizing Mary Shelley's monster, **The Curse of Frankenstein**. Christopher Lee, shortly to fill his face with fangs for Hammer's **Horror of Dracula**, now donned a proto-Beatle haircut and much mutilated-looking putty over his features to play the Creature. Hammer were restricted from using the copyrighted make-up devised by Jack Pierce for Karloff, and the difference tells. Lee merely looks as if he's been stung in the face by innumerable bees, and in his wrap-around neck-to-toe bandages he suggests a slimline Michelin Man who has gone mysteriously berserk.

None of Hammer's numerous Frankenstein movies – with Christopher Lee wisely yielding the monster's role to others, including Kiwi Kingston and Dave (Darth Vader) Prowse – boasted much distinction. But Hammer did usher in a new era of horror films, in which the old Gothic mists and chiaroscuro of the black and white films were replaced by meticulous sets and a vibrant color palette. Blood was now definitely

Above *Tippi Hedren can't hear herself scream as she is attacked by a murderous flock of misanthropic birds in Alfred Hitchcock's film* ***The Birds*** *(1963). Brilliant special effects and Hitch's suspense touch made this a thriller classic.*

blood, and not some ambiguously dark substance leaking from impaled persons.

Hammer also brought the Mummy back to cinematic life after a long lull. Christopher Lee once again donned the bandages and the lumbering gait for **The Mummy** (1959), and once again yielded them to others in the sequels.

Hammer's best ogre film was probably **Plague of the Zombies** (1966). Deep in eeriest Cornwall lives squire John Carson, lording it over a village and a tin-mine. What mysteriously efficient labor force he has harnessed to work this mine no one is sure – until the first sightings of pale and ghastly processions of walking corpses take place. John Gilling directs with flair, and the climactic scene of the village graveyard yielding up its dead – the blanched and bony hands reaching through the earth like hideous flowers, the pale verdigris faces rearing up – is Hammer at its best.

Who can know if this film inspired George Romero to direct the best zombie film of all, **Night of the Living Dead** (1968)? Shot in a ghostly, ghastly black and white, Romero's *walpurgisnacht* of the Undead, when risen corpses converge with murderous intent on an American small town, is magnificently unrelenting. It became, not surprisingly, a cult film and also begat a less successful color sequel by Romero, **Zombies – Dawn of the Dead** (1979).

It also helped create a terror climate in the cinema that gave rise to the faceless, stomping, implacable killer of John Carpenter's **Halloween** (1978) and the rash of such films that followed. Carpenter's killer is a psychopath who has escaped from the asylum where he has spent 15 years and wreaks violence on the town where he used to live. Like the zombie and the mummy, he has thus been "wakened" from a long inertia or hibernation. This is a feature so common to ogre stories in the cinema (Frankenstein and King Kong are

Right *George A. Romero's chilling zombie epic in black and white,* ***Night of the Living Dead*** *(1968), showed that low budgets can produce high-voltage horror. This was so good it became a cult film.*

THEY WON'T STAY DEAD!
An IMAGE TEN Production
NIGHT OF THE LIVING DEAD
They keep coming back in a
bloodthirsty lust for
HUMAN FLESH!...
Pits the dead against the living
in a struggle for survival!
Starring JUDITH O'DEA · DUANE JONES · MARILYN EASTMAN · KARL HARDMAN · JUDITH RIDLEY · KEITH WAYNE
Produced by Russel W. Streiner and Karl Hardman · Directed by George A. Romero · Screenplay by John A. Russo · A Walter Reade Organization Presentation — Released by Continental

Right and below *Flesh For Frankenstein* *(1974), directed by Paul Morrissey for producer Andy Warhol, showed us the cheerful side of dismemberment and surgery. The monster and his bride are comelier here than in earlier films, even though Frankenstein (Udo Kier) prefers operating with his eyes shut.*

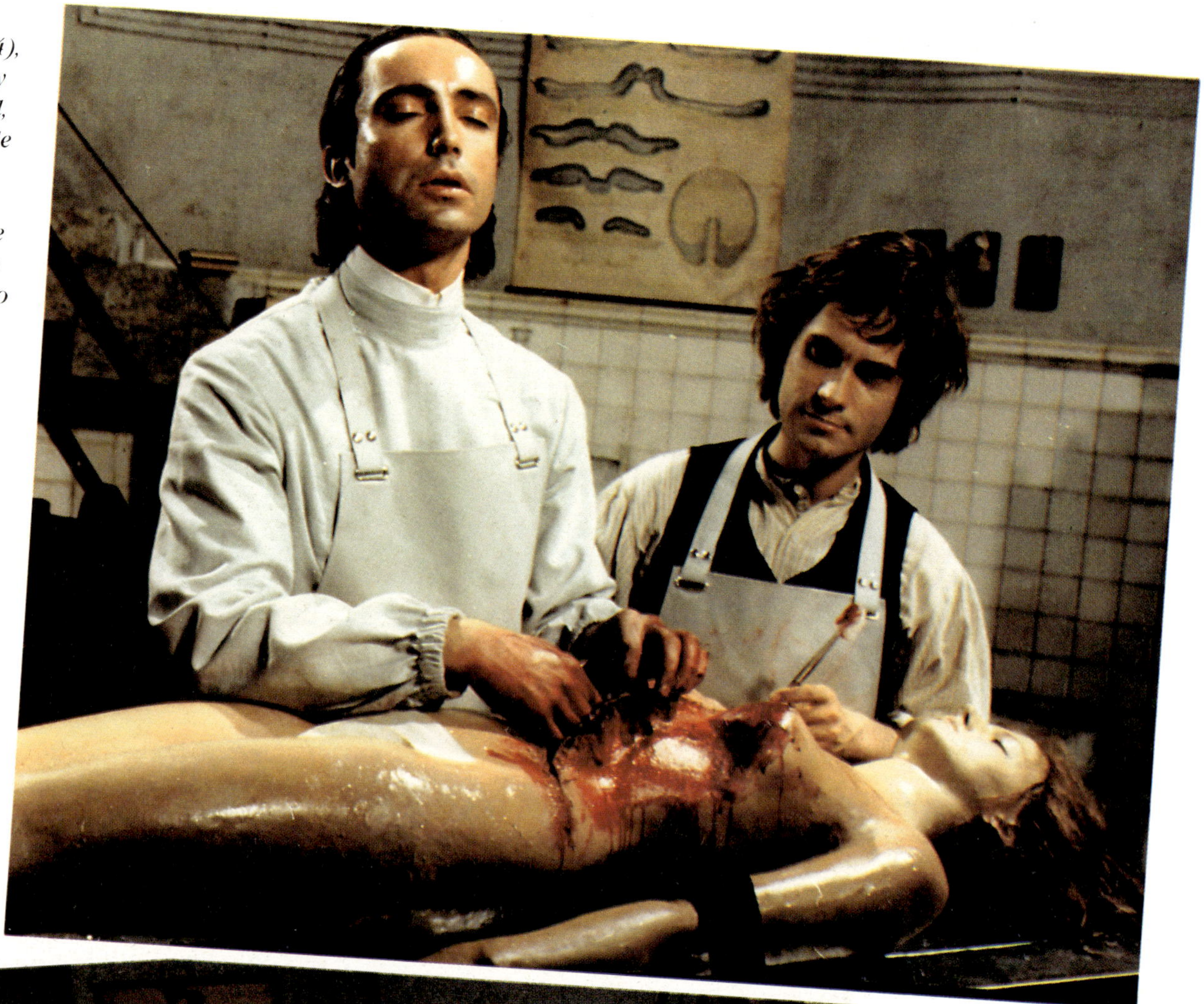

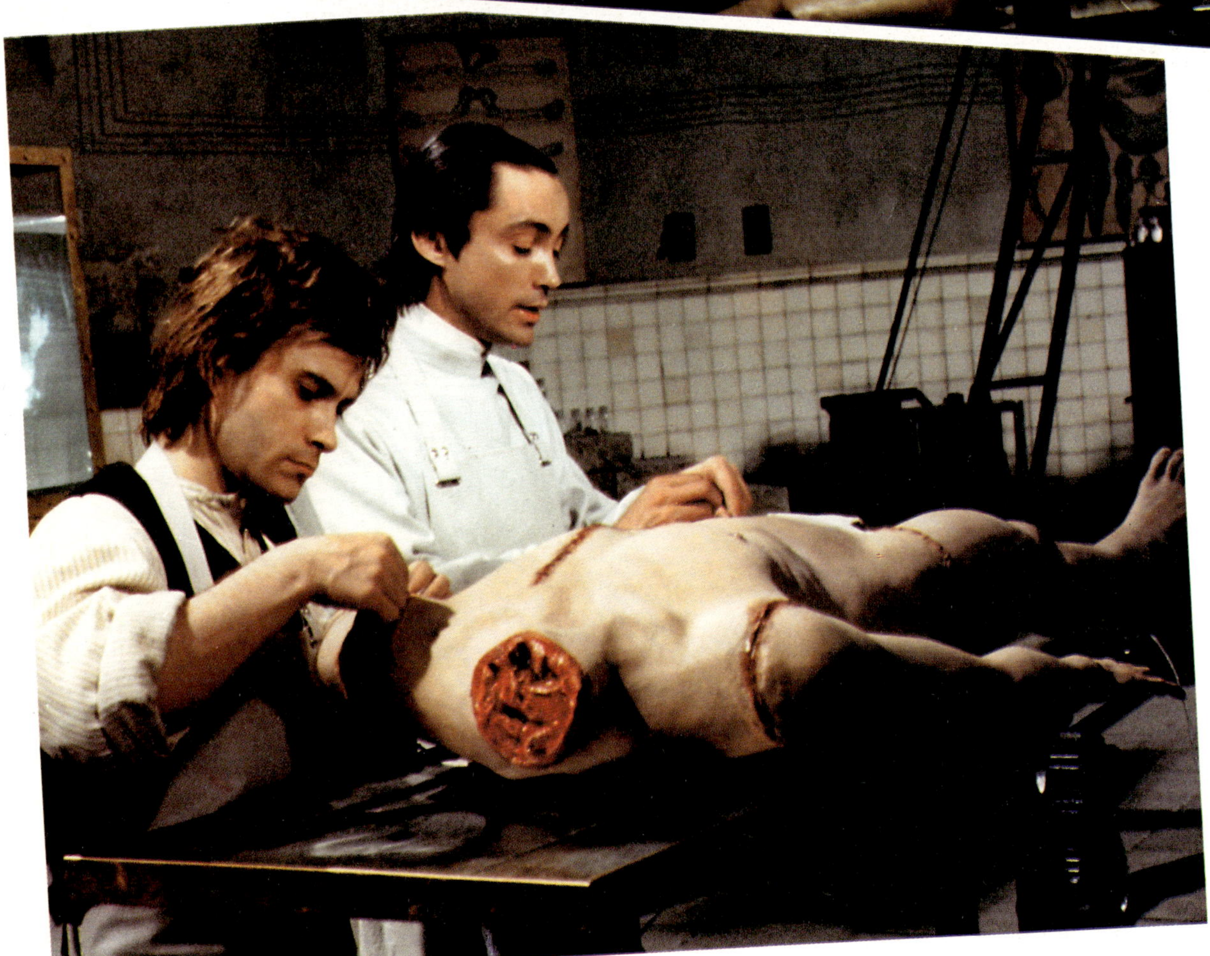

Above *Fun in the four-poster. Yvonne De Carlo and Fred Gwynne share an animated moment in TV's spoof-horror series* ***The Munsters.*** *A film,* ***Munster, Go Home*** *(1966), was also made.*

similarly "woken", one from the immobility of the laboratory table, the other from a time-warp island in the South Seas) that it's worth a closer look.

I suggested earlier that the ogre was a symbol for our fear of sudden, brutal, violent death, just as the occupier (Dracula and his chums) symbolized the slower, more insidious death of disease or illness. But both figures also symbolize the horror that can result from our attempts to *cheat* death. Frankenstein (the man, not the monster) attempts to cheat the laws of life and death by creating new life himself. The vampire attempts to cheat death by clinging to a grisly, parasitic hinterland between life and the grave. When these figures rear up before us, it's not only to rattle the grim specter of death before us but also to warn us to accept our fate rather than try to tamper with the intransient laws of mortality.

Twilight world

The zombie, of course, is merely a more palpable version of our old friend the ghost – in French the *"revenant"*, or "he who returns". And note how often in horror sequel titles two words keep cropping up: The Curse (of Frankenstein or the Mummy or the Cat People...) and the Return (of Frankenstein or the Mummy or..). For the curse *is* the return. The curse is to be woken from a long sleep – the finality of death – and roused to go and shake a finger, rattle some chains and generally read the supernatural riot act to human beings who think they can outwit the Grim Reaper. And the horror for human beings is to be confronted with the gruesome pain, misery and servitude of those either roused from peace or trapped in a twilight world between life and death.

As noted before, the zombie is a figure partaking of both the ogre and the occupier. He's a creature of stomping, implacable menace (ogre) and he's also one

of the twilight-undead ever driven to seek new recruits (occupier).

It's this ambivalence that makes the zombie – or the zombie-like killer – such a popular horror icon today. We've put aside the simplified Gothic polarities of Dracula and Frankenstein for the moment, and we seek something more compound and complex; not an ogre *or* an occupier, but an ogre-occupier.

Which also helps to explain the werewolf's new popularity. While definitely being an ogre – you can be in no doubt of the hairy beast's malicious intentions as with teeth bared, fur bristling, and headlights shining, it thunders towards you – the werewolf is also a recruiting creature like Dracula and an occupier. One bite and he has made you his for life – or at least for life-in-death.

And it's to the brigade of biters and the recruiters that we next turn...

Left *Do your loved ones return from the dead looking like this? In* ***Ghost Story*** *(1981) – starring Fred Astaire and (somewhere under the decay) Alice Krige – they do.*

Above *Zombies return – in George A. Romero's* ***Dawn of the Dead*** *(1979). In the ten years between* ***Night of the Living Dead*** *and this film, audience tastes had changed and Romero met the demand for more gore.*

3

The Silver Scream

As with the monster, so with the parasite – Germany got there first. Dracula made his first major film appearance, under another name, in F.W. Murnau's 1922 **Nosferatu.** (There was a 1913 film called **The Vampire,** directed by Sidney Olcott and Thomas Hayes Hunter, but it fell into immediate and lasting oblivion, as did Edison's one-reel version of **Frankenstein** in 1910. In terms of movie influence and evolution, the Frankenstein family tree begins with **The Golem** (1914), The Dracula family tree with **Nosferatu**.)

Not only the name was different, but the appearance too. Later generations of film fans have become used to the gaunt and gentlemanly charisma of Lugosi and Lee, who would both look entirely acceptably at a Lord Mayor's banquet (provided they didn't smile too much and reveal their excessive canines). But Max Schreck's Nosferatu is a hideous human whippet standing straight up in a frock-coat. Thin, long-fingernailed, rat-toothed, bat-eared and bald, he stands in the shadowy Gothic doorways of his castle like some fiend seeking sanctuary in the half-darkness.

Many of the later ingredients of movie Draculas, however, are here evident. He is a considerate host, he generously wines and dines his guests, he is as unobtrusive as possible when getting into and out of his coffins, and he attempts to win his victims by stealth and guile, never by violence.

An ordinary man

There is another aspect of **Nosferatu** which points the way ahead for movie vampiredom. It was shot almost entirely on location rather than in the claustrophobic and surreal studio sets then favored by Germany. So that this is the "unearthly" disguised as the everyday. And for all the Gothic trappings of later Dracula films – the cobwebbed castles, the Satanic cape, the midnight bat going bananas outside the window – the key to the Count's appeal is that he can just about pass himself off as an everyday Carpathian aristocrat: at least for long enough to entice his victims into his orbit and relax their guard.

Ironically, this ability of Dracula's to pass himself off as an ordinary chap – or at least an ordinary aristocrat – can sometimes result in horror movies so low-key as to create little horror at all. Hollywood's first **Dracula**, directed by Tod Browning in 1931, is an example. Though this is the film that started the whole vampire ball rolling, most of it is a dim and stagey tale of Count D (Bela Lugosi) wandering around London's high society and trading portentously wooden dialogue with the ladies whose necks he fancies. Based on a long-running Broadway stage version of Bram Stoker's novel, it is as creaking and formal as if Browning had merely pointed a camera at the stage from Row C in the theater stalls.

However, it did have a brief and darkly stylish prologue set in Dracula's castle – as sunset wakes the fiend and his fellows from their coffins – and it did have Bela Lugosi. This imperious gent with the glowing eyes, the gaunt, well-fed figure and the voice as rich, dark and tasty as Hungarian goulash, had a hypnôtist's charisma. He set the trend for future Draculas by speaking v-e-r-y s-l-o-w-l-y and fixing his victims with a basilisk stare before bending politely, inexorably, towards the neck.

Previous page *This shot from Werner Herzog's 1979 remake of* ***Nosferatu*** *perfectly captures the Count's stealthy insidious approach to his victims. Seconds later,* **below right**, *he is closing in on an unresponsive Isabelle Adjani, his teeth just inches away from her white neck.*

Right *F. W. Murnau's 1922 German classic* ***Nosferatu*** *gave the cinema its first great vampire story, based on Bram Stoker's book. Max Schreck played the bloodsucker.*

Below *Christopher Lee samples a neck in* ***Dracula AD 1972*** *(1972), his fifth outing as the Transylvanian terror.*

Nosferatu
PHANTOM DER NACHT
Imp G Darmon Paris

A village vampire

For all its imperfections, this first **Dracula** soon started pollenating the world. A year after its release, the Danish director Carl Dreyer made **Vampyr** (1932), another film seizing on the vampire's ability to camouflage himself in the everyday. Here there are no long-toothed demons in cape and evening wear, only a bizarre and increasingly macabre tale of unpleasant goings-on in a peasant village: a young traveler whose room has been mysteriously reserved for him at the inn, a one-legged gamekeeper building a coffin, an old man shot by an unseen bullet, a sick girl needing a blood transfusion, and a book entitled *Strange Tales of the Vampire* . . .

This masterpiece of fugitive, supersubtle menace typifies the vampire tradition's suavity as opposed to the blunt-instrument Gothicism of the ogre film. Vampire evil is so thin and rarefied it can steal into you like a mist or poison or miasma. Which didn't stop Hollywood, of course, trying to increase the melodrama in its sequels to Browning's **Dracula**, most of which were duly appalling: notably **Dracula's Daughter** (1936) and **Son of Dracula** (1943).

Indeed, the spirit of vampirism was most effective in these years when disseminating itself into *other* kinds of horror movie. The idea of the vampire as an evil, darkly majestic proselytizer, ever seeking new souls and bodies to enrol in his discipleship or capture as trophies, spreads to films like **The Most Dangerous Game** (1932), with Leslie Banks as the svelte and guttural Count Zaroff whose favorite sport is hunting down his guests with a pack of killer hounds, or like **White Zombie** (1932), with Lugosi lending his pale luminosity, gong-like voice and best evening clothes to the role of Caribbean zombie-master, or like those two "miniaturization" chillers, **The Devil Doll** (1936) and **Dr Cyclops** (1940), tales of quasi-vampiric power-mania and parasitism in which a "mad shopkeeper" (Lionel Barrymore) and a "mad scientist" (Albert Dekker), respectively, hold sway over a little army of six-inch human beings.

Everyday demons

But if we're scanning the horror cinema of the 1930s and 1940s for the themes of parasitism and possession – and looking for the occupiers rather than the ogres –

Below *Miniaturism runs riot in Tod Browning's* ***The Devil Doll*** *(1936), part of a great Hollywood tradition of sci-fi shrinkage that included* ***Dr Cyclops*** *(1940) and* ***The Incredible Shrinking Man*** *(1957).*

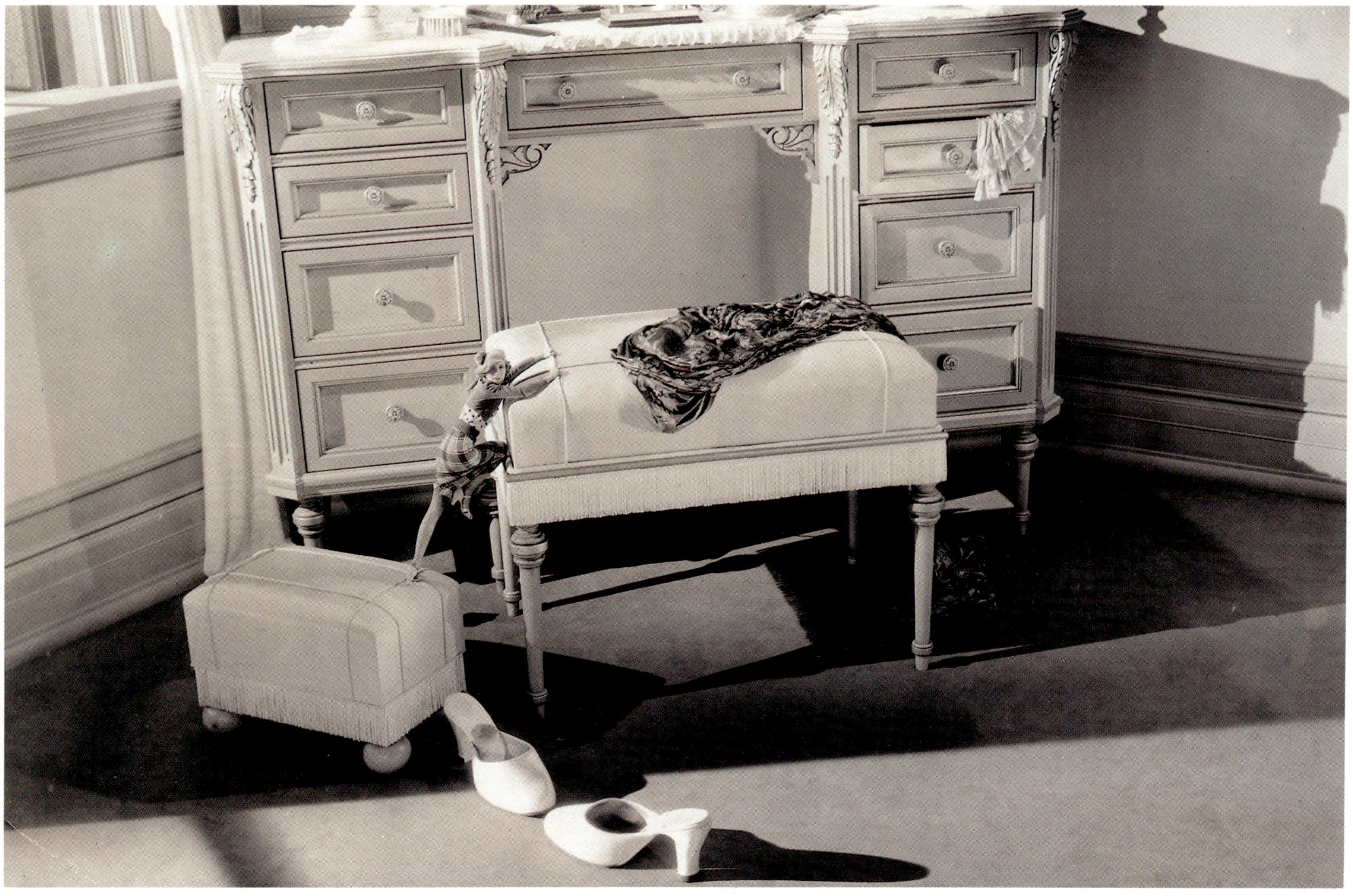

Above ***The Fall of the House of Usher*** *(UK, 1960) ushered in a whole series of atmospheric Edgar Allan Poe movies directed by Roger Corman and starring Vincent Price.*

one man's movies above all seize our gaze. Russian-born Hollywood producer Val Lewton made ten horror films for RKO in the 1940s. Though rejoicing in such penny-dreadful titles as **Cat People** (1942), **I Walked with a Zombie** (1943), **The Curse of the Cat People** (1944) and **The Body Snatchers** (1945), their style is eerie and elliptical, specializing far more in the menace of the unseen than in sledgehammer shock tactics. Like the vampire, Lewton's figures of evil are demons disguised in the everyday: a young girl who can turn into a jungle cat when her passions are roused, a West Indian planter's wife who just *might* be a zombie, and in **The Seventh Victim** (1943) a salon of rich, respectable ladies and gents in Greenwich Village who turn out to be devil-worshippers. The contagion of their evil is all the more dangerous for that, of course, and like Dracula their imperative is not only to survive with their own evil intact but to recruit other victim-acolytes to their cause.

The pace and pulse of Lewton's films are slow, deliberate, dreamlike. The shadowy visuals flatter and iridize – an indoor swimming pool stalked by an (unseen) panther, a waving West Indian cane field under a sickly moon – and everywhere horror is present, not as a sudden jack-in-the-box *éclat*, but as an ever-spreading miasma, reaching out into the night like the fingers of the shadows themselves.

The Corman canon

For the only comparable body of work in the movie horror canon we must jump twenty years and land with an enthusiastic thud on producer-director Roger Corman. Like Lewton, Corman never made a vampire film, yet vampiric themes – of parasitism, contagion, camouflaged evil and the twilight land between life and death – crowd the movies he made for American International Pictures in the 1960s, loosely based on stories or poems by Edgar Allan Poe, and starring (with one exception) Vincent Price.

In **House of Usher** (1960), Price twangs his velvety Gothic vowels as the haunted castle-dweller obsessed with the knowledge that his freshly coffined sister is still alive. Corman, Price and designer Daniel Haller capture a mood of Gothic melancholy, lurid decay and sickly unreason that Baudelaire – not to mention Poe –

would have been proud of. Using studio sets, and even studio-built exteriors (for Poe's forests, cliffs and misty tarns), Corman creates the most methodically claustrophobic series of horror films since the high noon (or dark midnight) of German Expressionism.

The pattern was repeated vividly and lividly in **The Pit and the Pendulum** (1961), **The Premature Burial** (1962), **Tales of Terror** (1962), **The Raven** (1962), **The Haunted Palace** (1963) and **The Masque of the Red Death** (1964). Only in Corman's last Poe venture did the magic disperse. **The Tomb of Ligeia** (1965), was shot on "real" locations in England (including a ruined Norfolk Abbey) and gone was the dreamlike asphyxiating landscape-of-the-mind that had been the Poe series' real strength.

Vincent Price in nearly all these films plays a kind of Dracula *manqué:* haunted and seigneurial, he dwells in the heart of his vast and cobwebbed domains, trapped on a filigree thread between life and death and catching every visitor in the toils of his own tragic longings. In the one Corman-Poe movie that Price doesn't appear in, **The Premature Burial** (he's replaced by Ray Milland), the temperature drops badly. For it's Price's hothouse preciosity, that velvet snarl and purr of a voice, that Gothic face riven with lines of esthetic doom and lunatic nobility, that help give Corman's films their grandeur.

Almost every film in the Dracula tradition, or located like the Lewton and Corman movies somewhere on the Dracula family tree, requires a castle or mansion. It's the little empire, cut off from the rest of the world, where the occupier can capture, quarantine, and play cat-and-mouse with his guest-victims. Only, of course, the "quarantine" area is for the purpose of infecting, not decontaminating, those guest-victims. No wonder that the Poe films – and the Lewton films and the Dracula films – are full of strange illnesses, sudden fevers, mysterious catalepsies, wasting weaknesses. (And in **Nosferatu**, both Murnau's 1922 movie and Werner Herzog's 1979 remake, the vampire brings a posse of plague-bearing rats to his new home-town on the Baltic.) As indicated in Chapter 1, part of the appeal of the occupier horror films is that they give mythic expression to – and also hopefully help to purge – our own fears of the slow, insidious and internal (as opposed to sudden, violent and external) face of death.

Also vital viewing in the annals of postwar horror – of the mysterious-miasmic rather than the monstrous variety – is the fitfully brilliant Italian school: Mario Bava's **Black Sunday** (1960) and **Blood and Black Lace** (1964), Riccardo Freda's **The Terror of Dr Hichcock** (1962), Michael Reeves and Charles Griffith's **The She Beast** (made in Italy under the title **La Sorella Di Satana**, 1965), and, above all, Dario Argento's **Suspiria** (1977). Set in a murder-prone girls' boarding school, Argento's glorious thriller of disembodied voices and diselemented shadows, sudden slashes of violence and surges of fear, is like a vampire thriller scripted by someone like Cocteau and designed by a latter-day Mondrian.

Right ***The Masque of the Red Death*** *(1964), seventh and most Bergmanesque of director Roger Corman's most haunting Edgar Allan Poe films.*

Left *One of the victims from Dario Argento's* ***Suspiria*** *(1977) who has just come to a sticky end.*

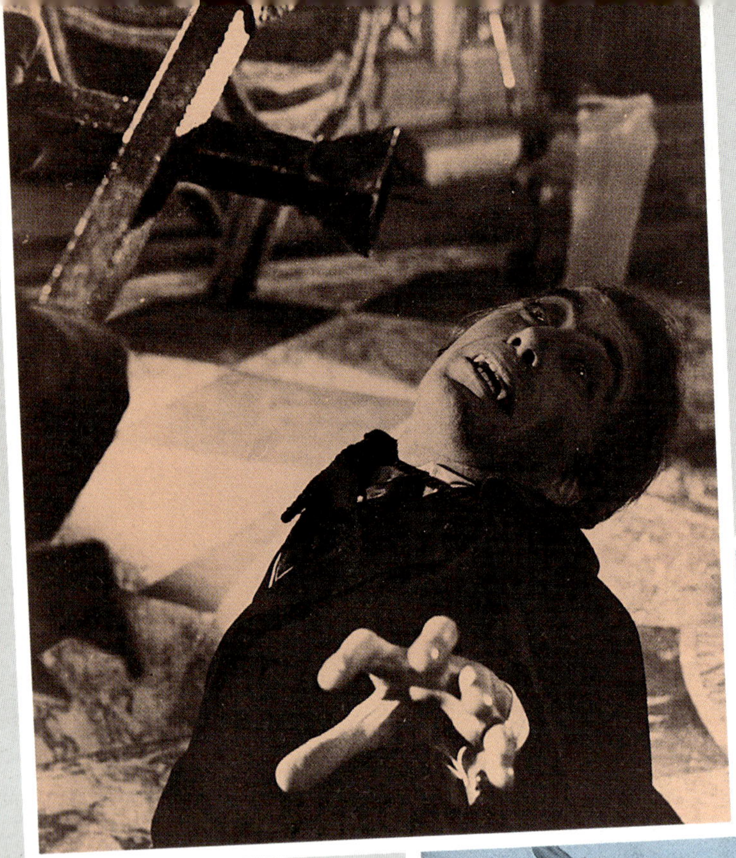

The British revival

Meanwhile, where was Dracula himself during all these years? The answer is that after a long time in the doldrums – neither the 1940s nor the early 1950s did anything to refresh, or even to maintain, his appeal – Dracula, like Frankenstein, was revived by Hammer Films. In the tall, gaunt and glacial person of Christopher Lee, he romped back to box-office acclaim in the 1958 **Horror of Dracula**. The film epitomized the Hammer horror style to come: handsome sets,

Top left *The plain man's guide to vampire disposal. Christopher Lee cowers before the cross as death approaches in Hammer's 1958* ***Dracula.*** **Above** *If crosses fail you can always tempt Dracula out onto the ice, and if possible through it, as in* ***Dracula Prince of Darkness*** *(1966).* **Left** *Christopher Lee considers his stake overdone in* ***Dracula Has Risen From the Grave*** *(Freddie Francis 1968). He rose four more times before Hammer finally closed the coffin.*

lashings of generous color (a novelty in a genre up to now favoring mist-wrapped black-and-white) and British actors elocuting sturdily through a well-crafted plot. Of magical ellipses *à la* Lewton, or poetic decay *à la* Corman, there was little or nothing. This was horror film-making as British as roast beef and two veg, with plenty of red gravy swimming around the dish.

That Hammer's Dracula films proved more effective than their Frankensteins is apparent in the greater number of sequels. There were five Frankenstein

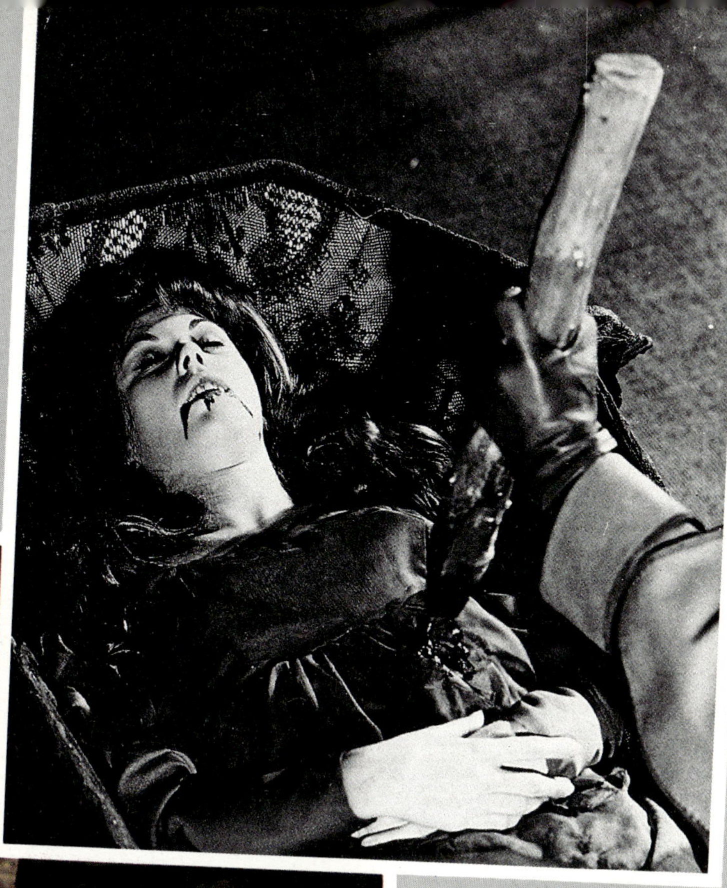

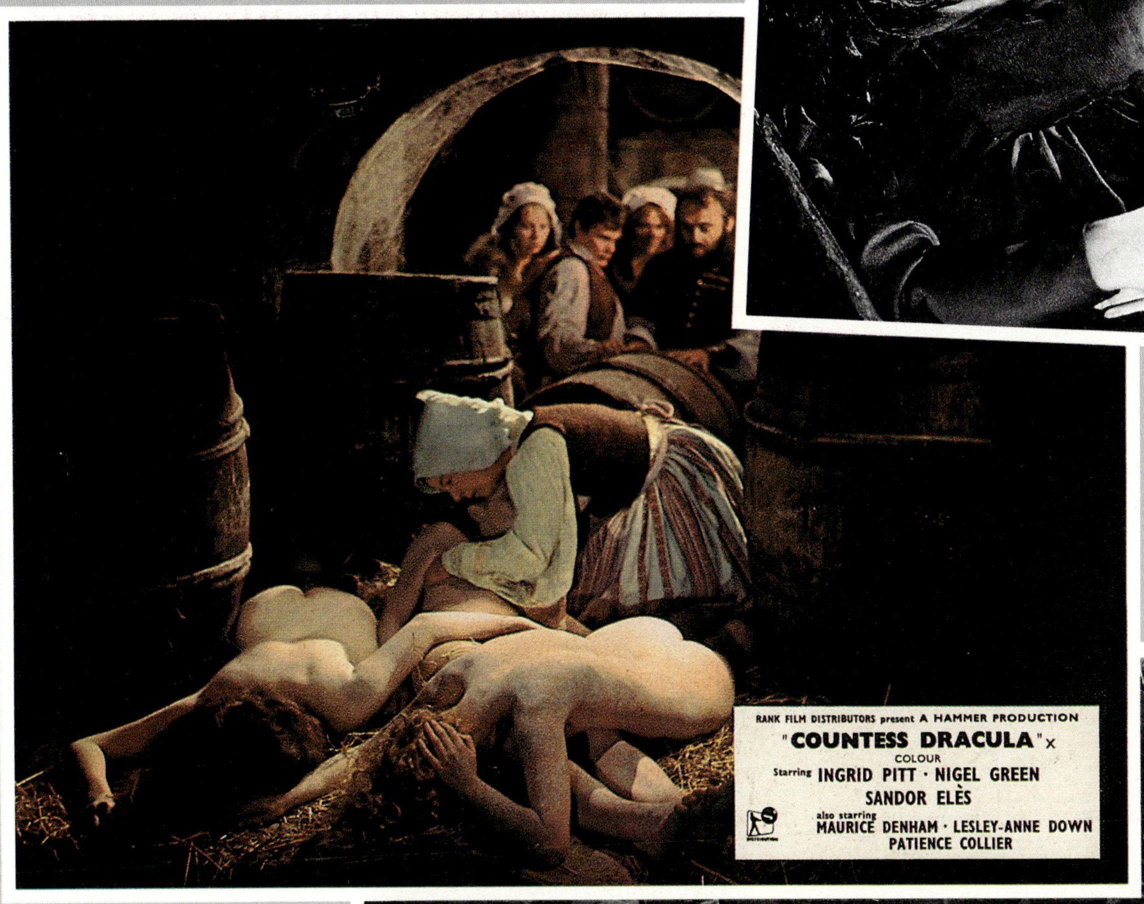

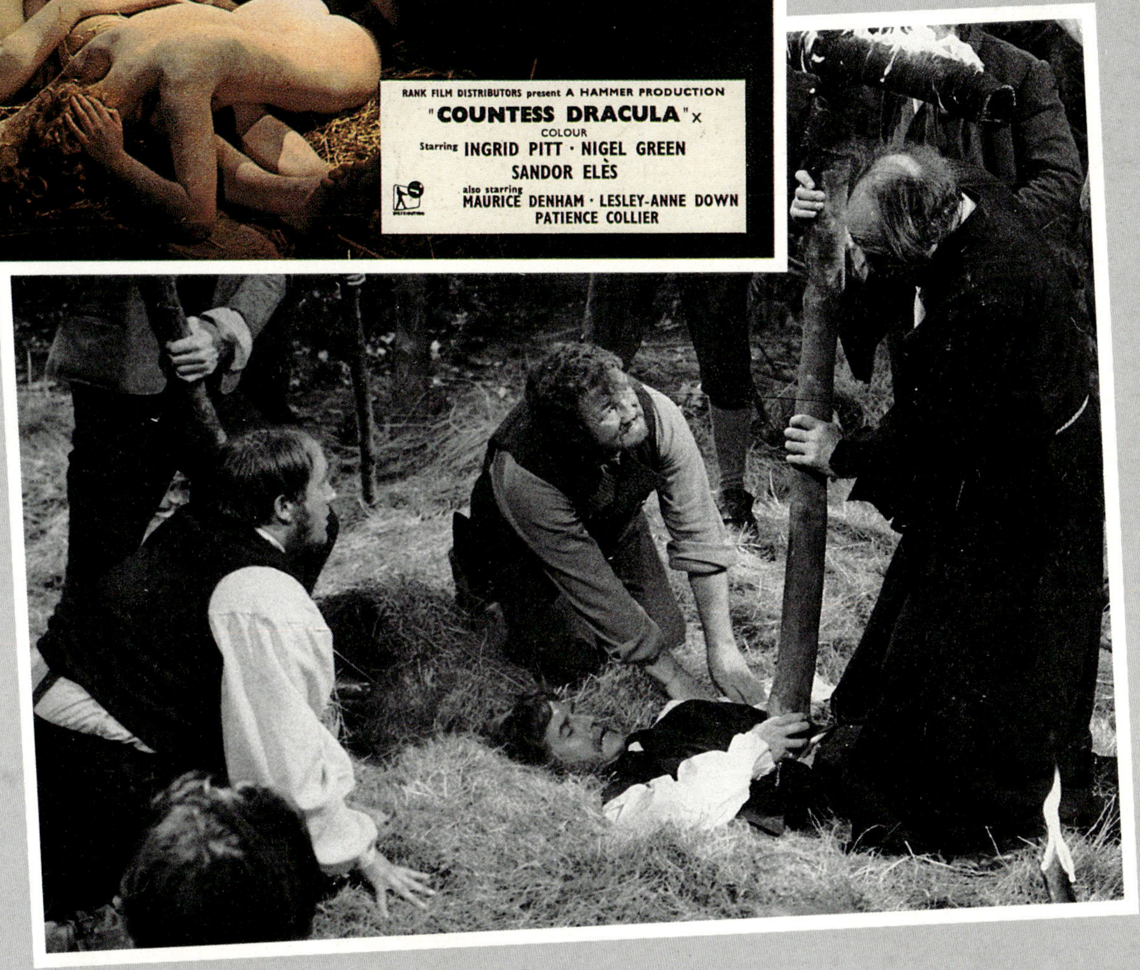

Top right *The gentler sex also need firm treatment when they become vampires. A stake in time in* **Countess Dracula** *(Peter Sasdy, 1970).* **Above** *A pile-up of the indefatigable Countess' victims. Hammer Films were always happy to cross the sex barrier in depicting horror icons.* **Right** *A devil-hunting priest in* **Tower of Evil** *(1974) believes in making doubly sure – not just a cross or a stake but both combined, with* flambé *effect thrown in.*

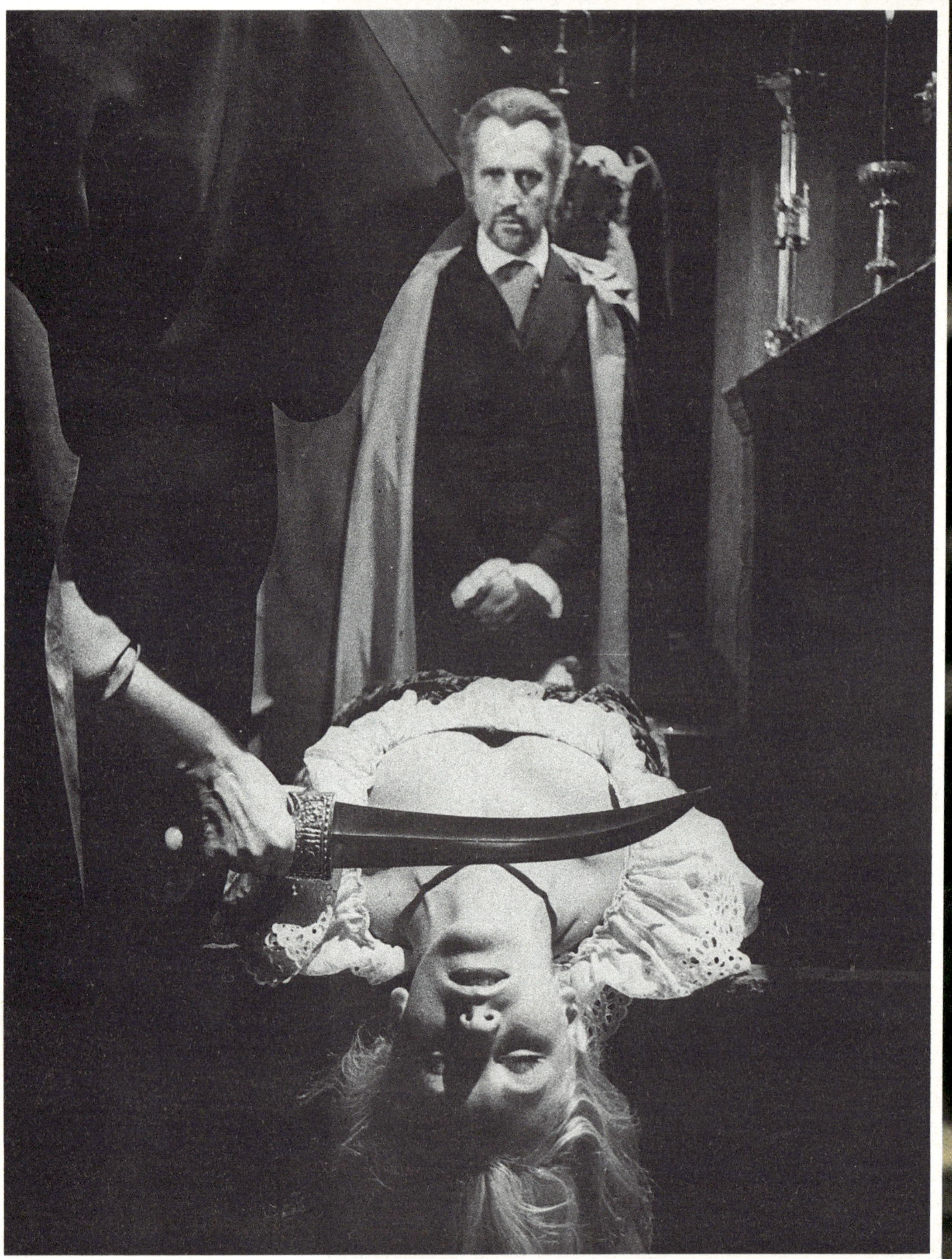

Above *Count Karnstein (Mike Raven) oversees a ritual sacrifice in Hammer's* ***Lust For A Vampire*** *(director Jimmy Sangster, 1971).*

Right *Vampirism goes canine in* ***Zoltan, Hound of Dracula*** *(1977).*

follow-ups, but Dracula notched up six direct sequels all starring Christopher Lee, plus a handful of indirect ones, from **The Brides of Dracula** (1960) to **Countess Dracula** (1971). Part of the explanation is Lee's own fitness for the role – the voice at once cultured and sepulchral, the face gaunt, Gothic, and palely glowing (thanks to Hammer's lighting cameramen) with a queasy luminosity. The rest of the explanation is probably the very "Britishness" of Dracula as a horror icon. After all, no *sang* could come more *froid* than that of this chilly aristocrat with his opera cape and impeccable manners: he sits somewhere on a sliding scale between Noel Coward and Lord Byron as a *bon viveur* with suavity, spotless sartorial style and crisply punctilious manners.

Furthermore, Hammer were not slow to cash in on the sexual possibilities of vampirism, which have always been a none-too-dormant part of the subject's appeal. No vampiric act can take place without intimate oral/dental contact, and the vampire has always preferred to operate through guile and seduction rather than uncouth coercion. So ladies soon climbed into the Transylvanian role, notably Ingrid Pitt who donned the mighty canines in **The Vampire Lovers** and **Countess Dracula** (1970) and purred her way to parasitic bliss while punctured necks multiplied in heaps around her.

And in eroticizing Dracula, Hammer proved oddly prophetic. For in the 1970s and 1980s, while one part

Above *Vampirism goes ethnic in* ***Blacula*** *(1972), a black spoof on the Dracula legend, directed by William Cain.*

Left *Ingrid Pitt, looking not a day over 200, counts her worry beads in* ***Countess Dracula*** *(1970). Immortality can be a great strain on the complexion.*

of the movie vampire tradition moved ever more nudgingly towards spoof and knockabout (**Vampira, Blacula, Love at First Bite** etc.), the other part turned Dracula into a prisoner of passion, a lost soul suffering the fires of love. In Hollywood's 1979 **Dracula**, directed by John Badham, Frank Langella's Count is no demon at all, but a velvet-voiced, palely languishing tragic figure consumed by love for Kate Nelligan. The vampire is similarly "humanized" in Louis Jourdan's portrayal for British television (1977). And in Werner Herzog's 1979 **Nosferatu the Vampire**, though you could hardly call Klaus Kinski's appearance (bald skull, pointed ears and rat teeth) "human", you were left in no doubt about the softer feelings inside the bloodsucker's hideous facade (Isabelle Adjani here being the recipient of the Count's more tender twinges).

Indeed, by the 1970s, the cinematic vampire was becoming such a polarized creation – you either had to laugh at him as a spoof or to sorrow for him as a wounded knight in love's lists – that it's no surprise he began to fall away as a credible horror protagonist. Themes of parasitism and possession – of the occupier as horror icon – began to spread instead into other movie legends and sagas (just as Frankenstein's monster had diversified into the zombie and the masked, faceless psychopath of the **Halloween** age).

Above *Mayhem, bondage and girls, girls, girls in* ***Dracula.*** *No self-respecting vampire movie is complete without a bit of garish Gothic S & M.*

Vomitorium visceralism

The most popular examples of the spreading empire of neo-vampirism were the **Exorcist**, **Omen** and **Amityville** films. Never has the idea of possession as a "disease" been more explicitly, not to say nauseatingly, presented than in **The Exorcist** (1973). Young Linda Blair, playing the Satanic occupee, breaks every rule of good social behavior from urinating on the carpet to emitting large quantities of spinach-green vomit. *En route* she masturbates with a crucifix, levitates her bed,

Right *Roman Polanski (who also directed) subjects Jack McGowan to dubious medical practices in the spoof horror* ***Dance of the Vampires*** *(1967).*

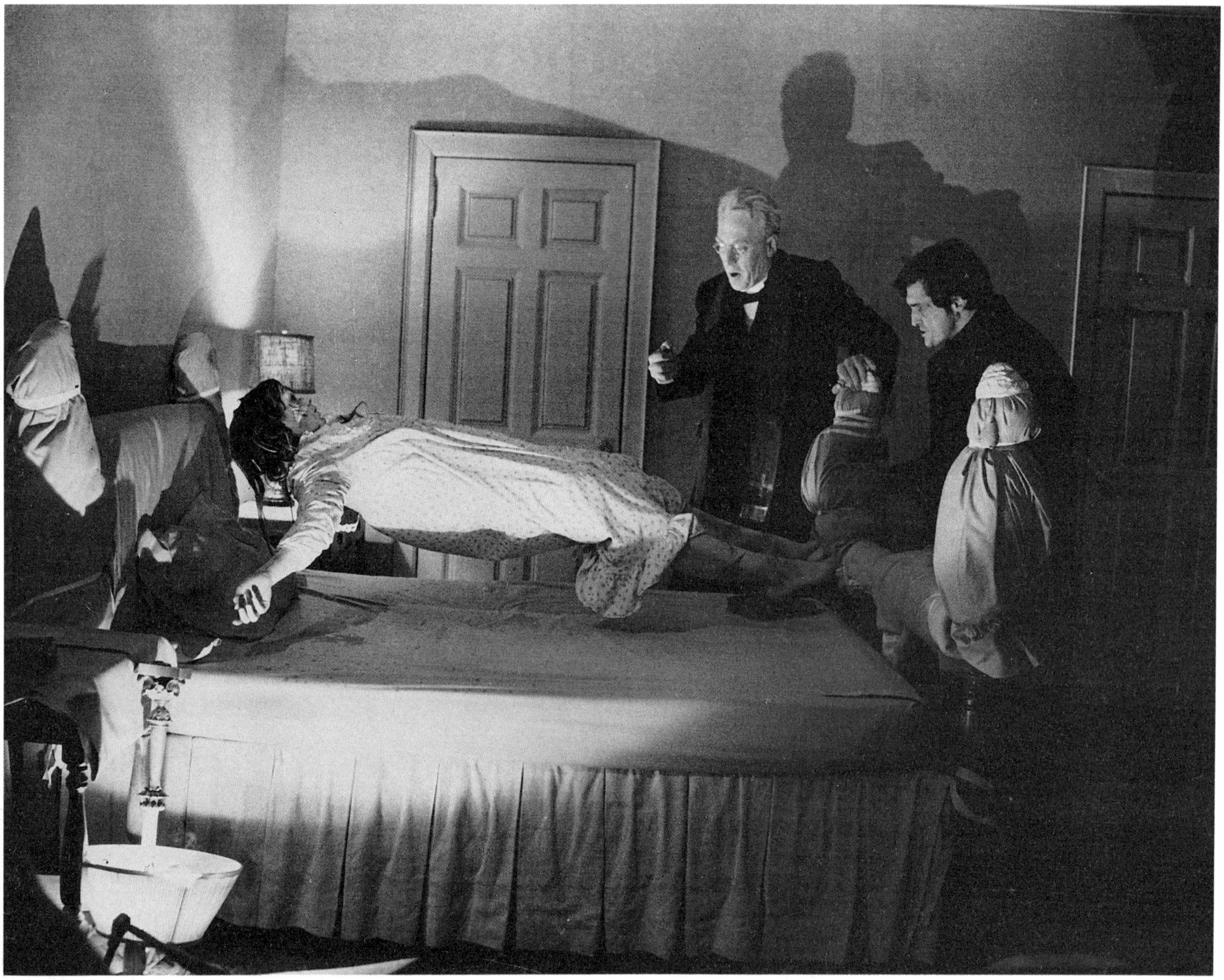

speaks with a voice deeper than Paul Robeson, and hurls a well-intentioned priest out of the window.

This Barnum and Bailey sensationalism yielded to a far subtler sequel in **Exorcist II: The Heretic** (1977), directed by John Boorman. But, for sinuous menace almost completely free from emetic special effects or vomitorium visceralism, we must go to **The Omen** (1976). Here the prowling menace of Satanic possession was seen in a series of bizarre illnesses and "accidents" – a hanging, a fall, a defenestration – linked by a narrative so cool, measured and macabre that it had all the flattering-to-deceive suavity of the best Dracula films. Its sequels fell away in quality, as the adventures of the "Antichrist" Damien (son of the U.S. Ambassador to Britain, Gregory Peck) gradually ran out of bright ideas for malevolence. But the **Omen** saga surpassed both the **Exorcist** saga and the later and progressively sillier **Amityville** series, in which Satanic horrors assail the successive owners of a house so grotesque and spooky-looking that no sane home-hunter would have bought it in the first place.

Above *Linda Blair levitates in **The Exorcist** (William Friedkin, 1974). Max Von Sydow and Jason Miller are the priests trying to bring her down to Earth.*

Right *The short sharp shock treatment. Gregory Peck finds a novel use for a pair of kitchen forks in the Satanic thriller **The Omen** (Richard Donner, 1976).*

One vital characteristic of the vampire and his ilk, of course, is that they are metamorphic. They can change the appearance and condition not only of their victims but of themselves, which is why such schizophrenic horror favorites as the werewolf, Dr Jekyll and Mr Hyde, and the protean heroine of **Cat People**, belong more properly to the Vampire Club than the Monster Club. It's also why, in the ambivalence-loving 1980s, all three terror icons have had favored treatment. Walerian Borowczyck's **The Blood of Dr Jekyll** (1981) is a brilliant *danse macabre* from the director of **Blanche** and **Immoral Tales** (1974), allowing the rhythms of

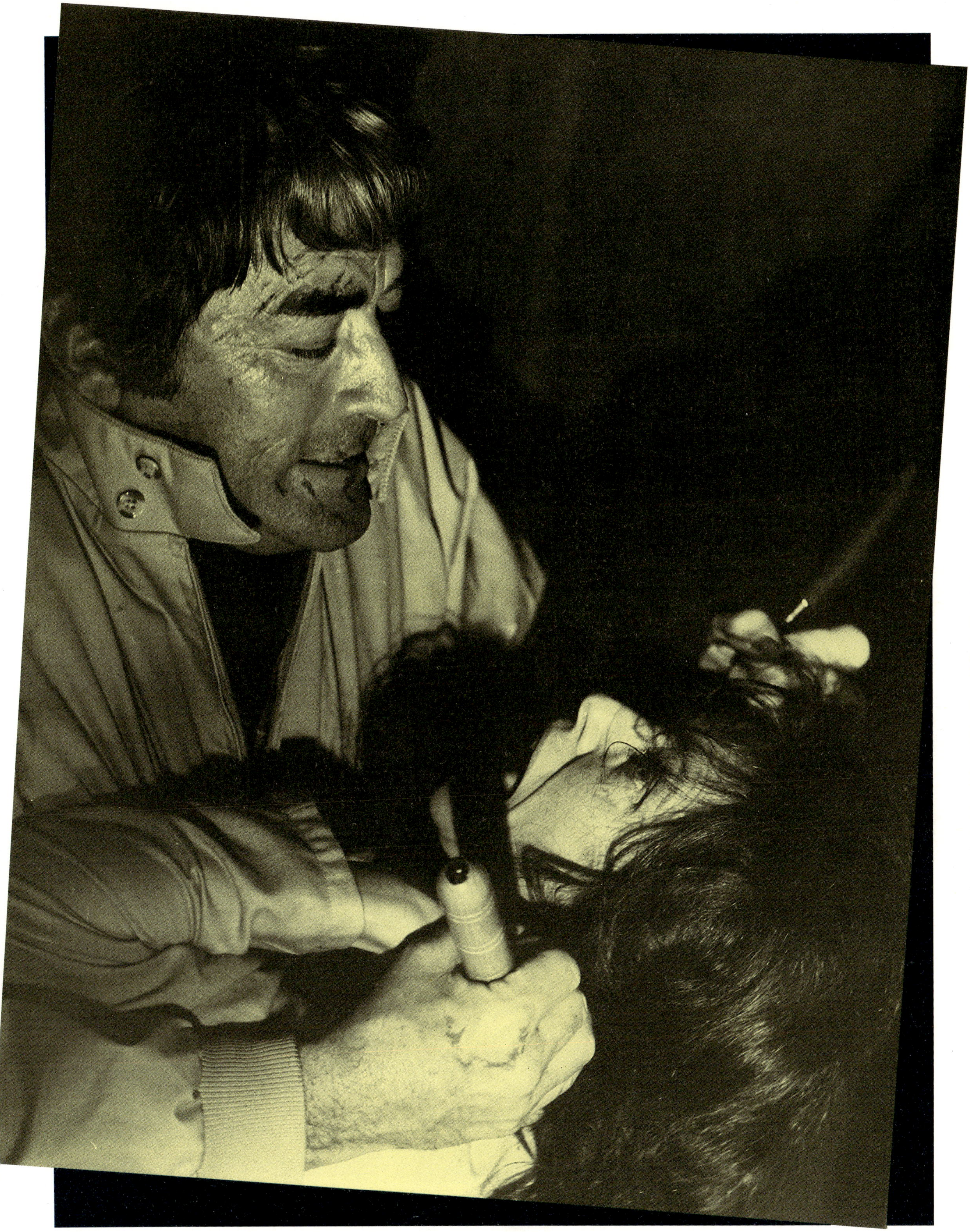

Left *Nastassia Kinski in a screaming mood in Paul Schrader's haunting 1982 remake of the 1942 Val Lewton film* ***Cat People.***

Below *A black panther (or is it Miss Kinski in feline form?) disturbs the sleep of John Heard.*

Above *Lupine confrontation in* ***The Howling*** *(1982). Werewolfery and special effects galore in this film, written by John Sayles and directed by Joe Dante.*

its hero's quick-change personality to spread out to the whole movie, a murder tale of lightning cuts, delirious shadowplay and sudden switches between horror and comedy. It's the perfect poetic consummation to eighty years of movie variations on Robert Louis Stevenson's schizoid shocker.

Paul Schrader's **Cat People** (1982) is a sinisterly potent remake of the 1942 original, at once lyrical and lethal as it steers Nastassia Kinski and Malcolm McDowell through a Gothic shadowland and the mazes of a modernized possession myth. And the werewolf, at whom we'll be looking more closely in the next chapter, has evolved spectacularly from the bad old Hollywood days when he tended to roam about resembling a growling ham actor who had been inadvertently tarred and feathered. Now, in films like **The Howling** (1981) and **The Company of Wolves** (1984) he's a triumph of realistic special effects and just about Top Demon in the modern horror canon.

In these films the kind of Satanic and predatory forces often neatly and potently concentrated in Dracula are diversified into a whole menagerie of ghouls, ghosts and long-leggedy (or short-leggedy) beasties. Dracula and Frankenstein are merely the crowned heads of their respective horror kingdoms. It's a vampiric version of Satanism, for example, that dominates Polanski's **Rosemary's Baby** (1968), with the idea of evil as a weakening illness sowing fever and hallucination. It's a vampiric version of homicidal psychopathology that dominates German director Ulli Lommel's **The Tenderness of Wolves** (1973) with its child-murderer (Kurt Raab) fond of embellishing his crimes by sucking his victims' blood. And it's even – and most ingeniously – a vampiric version of the Frankenstein legend that dominates the 1971 British horror film, written by Robert Wynne-Simmons with its director Piers Haggard, **Blood on Satan's Claw.** Here the Devil seeks to "assemble" himself for an earthly visit by furrily infecting different parts of different people's bodies: these parts to be cut away and then joined into the corporeal presence of Satan himself! The assembly-kit genesis of the promised monster is a clear echo of **Frankenstein,** but the theme of sly, plague-like demonic contagion belongs to the Dracula tradition.

At the end of the 1960s – which was also the end of Hammer's reign as the last determined perpetuators of Dracula and Frankenstein as distinct legends – horror divisions were clearly crumbling and horror archetypes could begin to crossbreed in the fertile anarchy that resulted. In the 1970s it was open season for filmic horror-hunters. And in the 1980s that open season has begun to look alarmingly like a bloodbath…

4
Horror 1980s Style

The Dracula and Frankenstein stories have the simplicity of great archetypes. One is predicated on the belief that there is such a thing as suave, Byronic, even "gentlemanly" evil; the other on the belief that violence can be blind, mindless and inexorable, a steamroller punishment set in motion by Fate, with its agent almost as doomed and helpless a figure as his victims.

The 1970s, and even more the 1980s, have found these grand undiluted archetypes unacceptable – except as primary colors with which to mix other horror icons and images. To suit our tastes, Dracula and Frankenstein must either be made more human and join the complex throng of human suffering (as in John Badham's 1979 **Dracula**, or Jack Smight's TV-made **Frankenstein – The True Story,** 1973, scripted by Christopher Isherwood) or else have their Gothic simplicities shaken up completely by a visit to the spoof merchants (Mel Brooks and Co.).

But while Dracula and Frankenstein are being thus rehabilitated, what of our abiding taste for demons and monsters, occupiers and ogres, which must be satisfied in the interim? The answer is that large chunks of these legends, and of the themes and motifs that constitute their appeal, are to be found scattered through the horror movies of the last fifteen years.

Take teeth. Teeth have been a vital part of horror mythology through the ages. No vampire or werewolf, no leopard man or cat person, could possibly present himself in public without a good set of man-eating – or at least man-biting – molars. They're the human body's knife, and their principal terror property is that they're concealed – at least with vampires – behind the human body's softest, most ingratiating part, the mouth. So the lethal canines behind the smiling lips are the human anatomy's answer to Chaucer's "smiler with the knife under the cloak".

Teeth are thus the perfect heraldic weapon of the vampire, who camouflages his evil intentions with the courtly welcome of the perfect host.

So when Dracula went into filmic decline, what happened to his teeth? Try **Jaws** (1975). Then try **Alien** (1979). Then try **Gremlins** (1984). The snappers are alive and well and living in other Hollywood myths. But there's a difference you will notice too. The gentlemanliness has gone completely. There is no Byronic charisma about the shark in **Jaws**; you would never agree to be wined and dined in his Gothic castle (if he had one) by the Alien; and I doubt if the Gremlins would considerately have a bedroom made up for you before they bit you in the neck.

Previous page
Bloodthirsty moment from Neil Jordan's ***The Company of Wolves*** *(1984). Werewolves, after a fitful previous life in the cinema, have roared back into fashion since 1980.*

Altering states

What *is* retained from the Dracula tradition, however, is the motif of camouflage and the metamorphic appearance or personality of the assailant. The shark in **Jaws** is almost a mystery presence until the movie's climactic chase: screened by the ocean, he erupts only in bloody flourishes so quick they deceive the eye. And much of Steven Spielberg's film is taken up with rancorously impassioned debates as to how big the shark is. So that, though the fish does not *literally* change shape and personality before our eyes, in our imagination it is in constant flux.

In **Alien**, the title creature, sowing panic aboard a spaceship, *does* change shape as the film proceeds. Its first bout of activity is as a hideous "thing" bursting out of John Hurt's chest – it gives a strangled cry and resembles a skinned hybrid of lamb and snake – but its before-and-after manifestations also include an immobile, face-sucking polyp and a six-foot scaly monster with slavering teeth and retractable jaw.

As it ambushes the crew one by one and eats them, the Alien is also, vampirically, a master of camouflage. It hides in dark corners, it borrows color and texture from its surroundings, and it shocks the life out of us near the end by uncoiling from the very pipes and wires of a spaceship wall.

The marauding mischief of the **Gremlins** offers one of the best recent comic – or horror-comic – variations on vampirism. These lethal and toothy creatures pounce upon an unsuspecting American small town after first presenting themselves in the guise of cuddly pets, offspring of the appealing little "Mogwai", a sort of long-eared Pekinese, which inventor Hoyt Axton buys for his teenage son (Zach Galligan). Like Dracula, these creatures first insinuate themselves into their victims' good graces and then – metamorphosing with a little help from a midnight snack – bare their lethal teeth and their ravening Ids.

Of course, these predators – the shark, the alien, the gremlin – are far redder in tooth and claw than Dracula ever was. But it's the privilege of each generation of horror fans to respond to, or even demand, changes in the old archetypes. Social history and movie history always evolve in close parallel; and sociologists and critics have long held that the rash of 1950s films about extraterrestrial invasion and humans turning into "pod people", for example (like **Invaders from Mars**, 1953, and **Invasion of the Body Snatchers**, 1956),

Above *Terror in the briny. Steven Spielberg's* ***Jaws*** *(1975) found new directions for the dental menace of vampirism. The snapper in full cry with,* **(inset)** *a sample victim.*

Left *It'll be all bite on the night. A gremlin in monstrous mood from* ***Gremlins*** *(1984).*

Right *Mel Brooks pokes fun at Grand Guignol in* ***Young Frankenstein*** *(1975). Gene Wilder played the mad scientist, Peter Boyle his monster, and the Frankenstein genre hasn't recovered yet.*

Below *Since the early 1970s horror films have been under spoof-attack from all sides.* ***The Rocky Horror Picture Show*** *(Jim Sharman, 1975), based on the stage musical, scrambled together every horror tradition from Dracula and Frankenstein to the Old Dark House. The result became a cult hit in every late-night cinema.*

were a reflection of Cold War paranoia and Commie-phobia during the McCarthyite era. Similarly, Siegfried Kracauer in his book *From Caligari to Hitler* insists that the horrors of 1920s German Expressionism were symptomatic of the prevailing alarmist climate that allowed Hitler to rise to power.

For the critic gazing at horror films in the 1970s and 1980s it's not too fanciful to see echoes of Vietnam in the guerrilla-style horrors of **Alien** – that spine-chiller of concealed sudden ambush – or even in the rending eruptions from apparent peace of **Jaws**. Indeed, Harlan Kennedy in his ingenious and perceptive *Film Comment* article on modern horror films, "Things That Go Howl in the Id", argues exactly that – and also detects signs of Watergate and Nixon-phobia in the late 1970s rush of werewolf films (Richard Nixon being not bad casting for any Big Bad Wolf character around).

What is fascinating about the post-1960s horror film, however, is that for all its mutations and crossbreedings it still retains a vestigial division between "ogres" and "occupiers", the Frankenstein family and the Dracula descendants. Where the latter thrive by stealth, subterfuge, camouflage and parasitic ambush (the Alien in its early manifestations is almost literally a parasite, first feeding on John Hurt's face and later dwelling in his bowels), the Frankenstein heirs still favor the mask-like face, the stomping implacable walk and the use of the crudest, most primitive weaponry around. Knives, cleavers, harpoons, hammers – you name it, they are happy to use it.

Madmen on the loose

The two main exercise grounds for the post-1960s ogre have been the **Halloween** and **Friday the 13th** series. In John Carpenter's 1978 horror romp, which piloted the first series, it's Halloween day in small-town America and an escaped lunatic is on the prowl. For most of the film we only see him in glimpses, a totemic menace materializing on streets in broad daylight. But when he finally stomps into center screen – with that hideous masked head, that ineluctable walk, that tendency to crash unceremoniously through doors or windows – we know this is Frankenstein 1970s-style.

The stalking killer in the **Friday the 13th** saga is no less brutal and often no less camera-shy. Indeed, for most of the 1980 movie and its sequels, rather than appearing in front of the camera he takes refuge in *being* the camera as it judders through woods and clearings, breathing heavily and loudly snapping twigs and breaking branches. (One sometimes feels that if the murder charges didn't stick to this killer, one could have him up for criminal defoliation.)

A crucial characteristic of the Frankenstein family, and one shared by these killers, is intellectual subnormality. Unlike the intelligent and even sophisticated Dracula family, they are mentally maimed or retarded. The killer in **Halloween** is an escaped madman and "Jason", the persevering slayer of **Friday the 13th**, has a mind unhinged by bereavement and crazed by a robotic call to vengeance. As indicated in an earlier chapter, you can reason with a vampire – though he will probably out-reason you or simply out-maneuver you – but the only way you can reason with an ogre is by using a blunt or sharp instrument.

Teenage traumas

Not content with marching grimly through these money-spinning scream sagas, the neo-Frankenstein style of killer appeared in a veritable epidemic of

Above *Just one of the ghoulish sights on your ride through* ***The Funhouse*** *(1981), a fairground screamer directed by Tobe (****Texas Chainsaw Massacre****) Hooper.*

bloodbath horror films in the 1970s and early 1980s. Their linking characteristic – common to such as **Prom Night** (1980), **Terror Train** (1980) **Hell Night** (1981) and **Splatter University** (1984) – is that they favored student environments. The victims were teenagers from schools or colleges and the killer could be anything from a slighted fellow-pupil (**Terror Train**) to a mad headmaster (**Splatter University**). Almost invariably, the killer would manifest himself in ghoulish incognito – hideous masks favored – and do his murderous bidding by the most crudely picturesque methods available. Nothing so simple and subtle as a gunshot could be permitted when the alternatives might be a meat-hook, a scythe or a cleaver.

The founding father of the post-1960s blood-and-guts horror film is undoubtedly Tobe Hooper's **The Texas Chainsaw Massacre** (1974). Here a group of teenagers are driving across Texas in a dormobile when it runs out of petrol. (Only think how many horror films we'd lose if motorists always made sure they had a full tank.) One by one, or pair by pair, they walk over to the sinister white clapboard mansion standing on the twilight skyline nearby – and one by one, or pair by pair, they are horribly done to death, except for the last surviving girl (Marilyn Burns) who manages to escape the terrors of hammer and chainsaw and dash to the safety of the highway.

Above *"Doctor, I have this terrible headache..." A not-for-the-squeamish moment from one of the blood-and-gore epics popular in the 1980s,* ***House By The Cemetery*** *(1981).*

The movie's chief ogre is a slaughterhouse Frankenstein: a lumbering brute in mask and blood-spattered apron who, with a little help from his family, operates this roadside human abattoir. Choice "cuts" from his victims end up in the nearby petrol station *cum* rotisserie. Murder methods include impaling victims on a meat-hook, bashing their heads in with a hammer (this is Grandad's favorite) or chasing after them with the eponymous and loudly-buzzing chainsaw.

No stomach is left unturned by Hooper's movie. But whether you like the modern trend towards upchuck visceralism or not, it has become such a dominant feature of recent horror films that it can't be ignored in any survey of the genre.

The big throw-up

Canadian director David Cronenberg has made a virtual one-man industry out of encouraging us to reach for a brown paper bag. Audiences who thought **Rabid** and **Shivers** revolting enough soon had another think coming with **Scanners** and **Videodrome**. The first

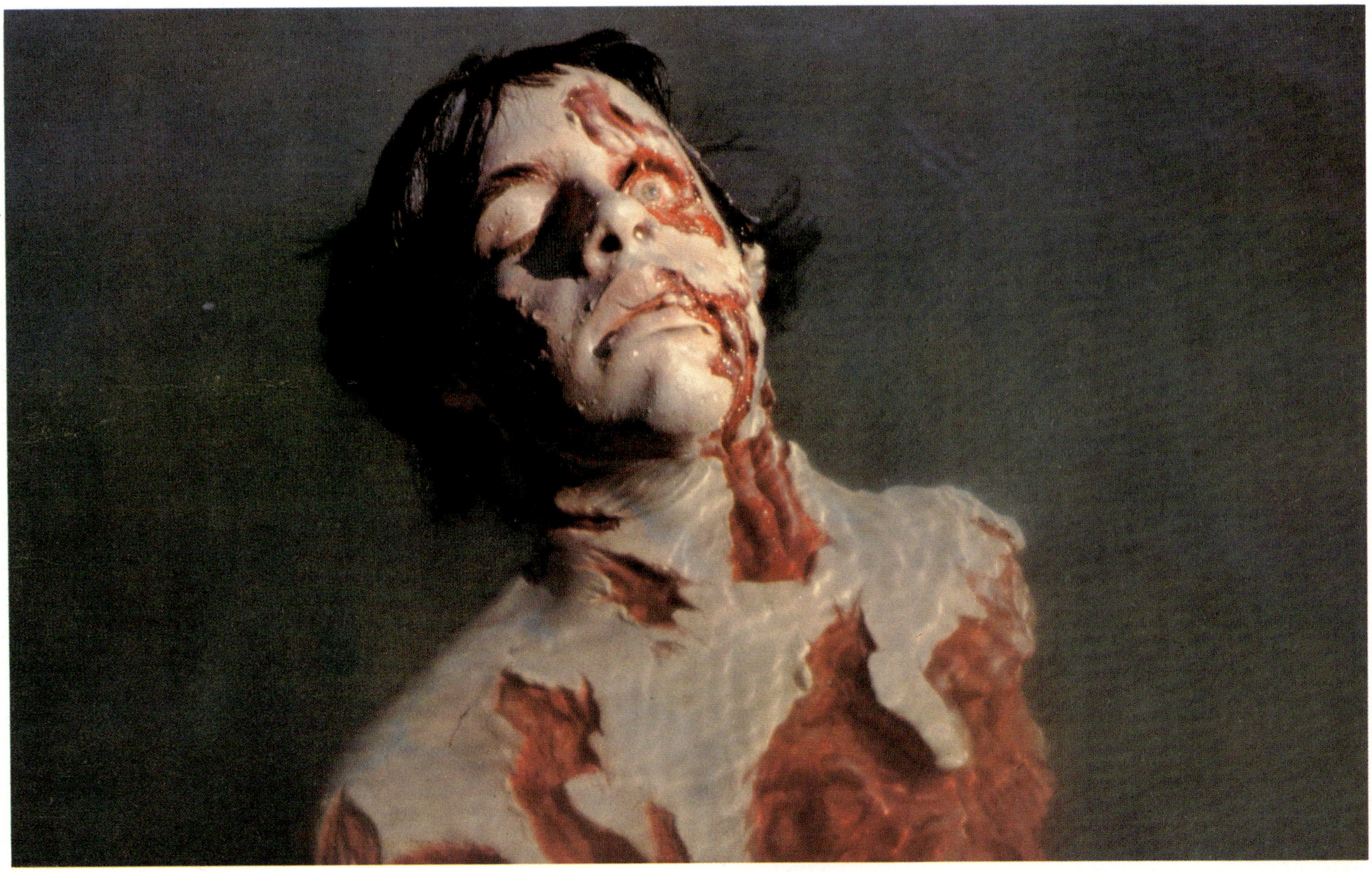

Above *Fishing can seriously damage your health, as this victim discovered in Joe Dante's* ***Piranha*** *(1978). John Sayles (of* ***The Howling****) wrote the witty, mischievous script.*

Right *David Cronenberg's* ***Rabid*** *(1977) had grisly moments, but he was to outdo himself later in* ***Scanners*** *(1981) and* **(overleaf)** ***Videodrome*** *(1982) an ambitious film where objects become flesh and flesh objects.*

has people's heads splitting apart, spouting blood or simply exploding: the second has a man's stomach turning into a human video-recorder, opening a large vulva-like gash into which one inserts one's favorite cassettes. (But not, I think, **The Sound of Music**.)

John Carpenter's **The Thing** takes Howard Hawk's same-name sci-fi thriller of 1951 and remakes it for the gory 1980s. Mutilations and mutations occupy about equal screen time, as a group of Arctic scientists are picturesquely torn apart by alien forces. A decapitated head sprouts spider legs and scuttles across a floor; a dog's head spontaneously bursts open like a bloody flower; and the climax features the "thing" itself, a towering, roaring, slavering bouquet of limbs and innards and organs all lashing around like an escaped Hieronymus Bosch painting.

Visible violence

The trend to visceralism has reached its grisly apogee in the series of horror movies lumped together – in Britain at least – under the heading "video nasties". Some of these were made originally for the big screen, some for the small, but most directly for the video market. But all – in the opinion of Britain's appointed censors and self-appointed moral crusaders – are so graphic in their depiction of violence or brutality that

Below *"Not where he eats but where he is eaten" (Shakespeare, "Hamlet"). Four grisly characters dine on a fifth in* ***Zombie Flesh-Eaters*** *(1979).*

Right *Looks harmless enough, doesn't it? But this poor girl in* ***Zombie Flesh-Eaters*** *is about to have her eye impaled on a large splinter. In full color – and in close-up.*

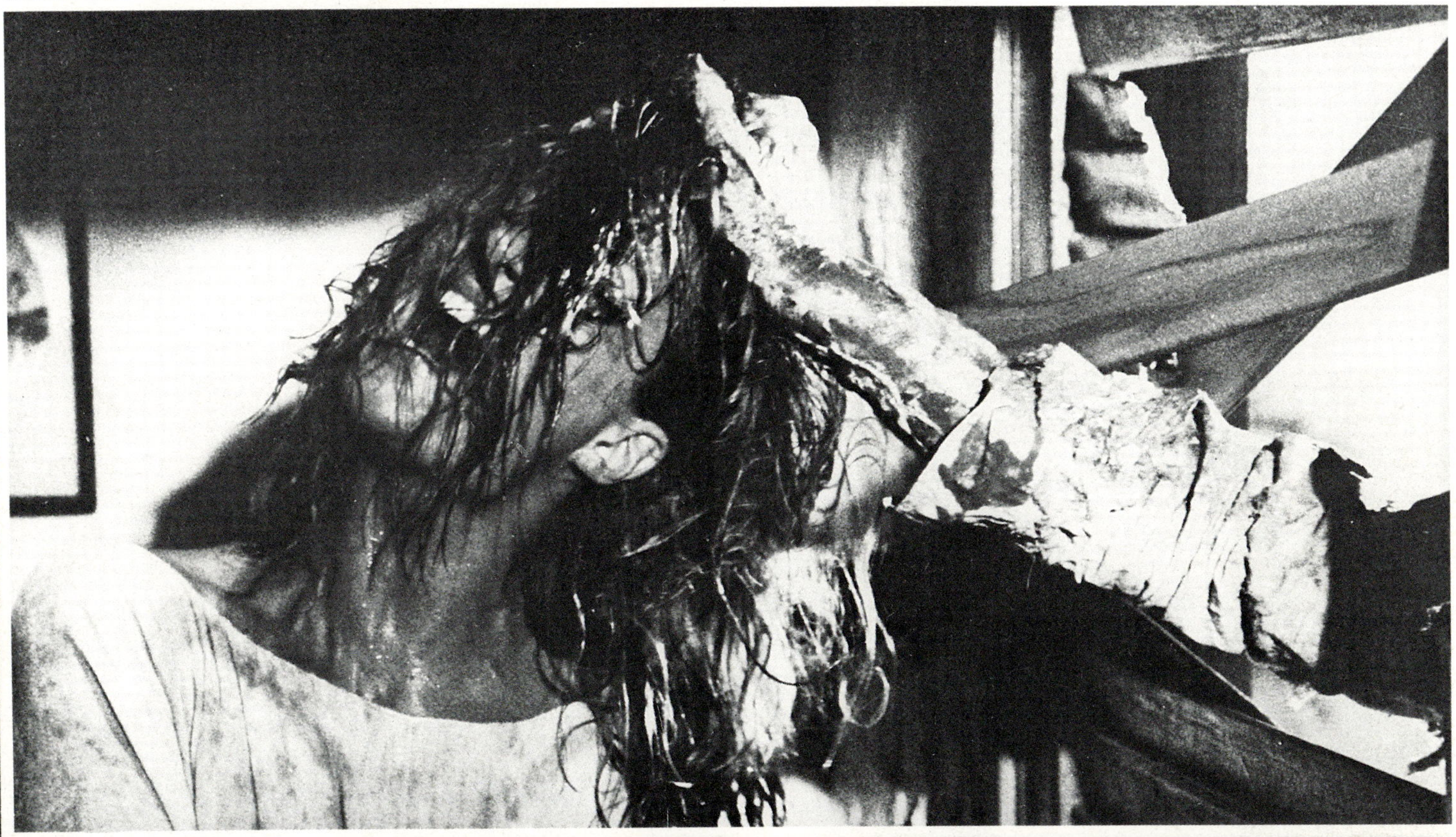

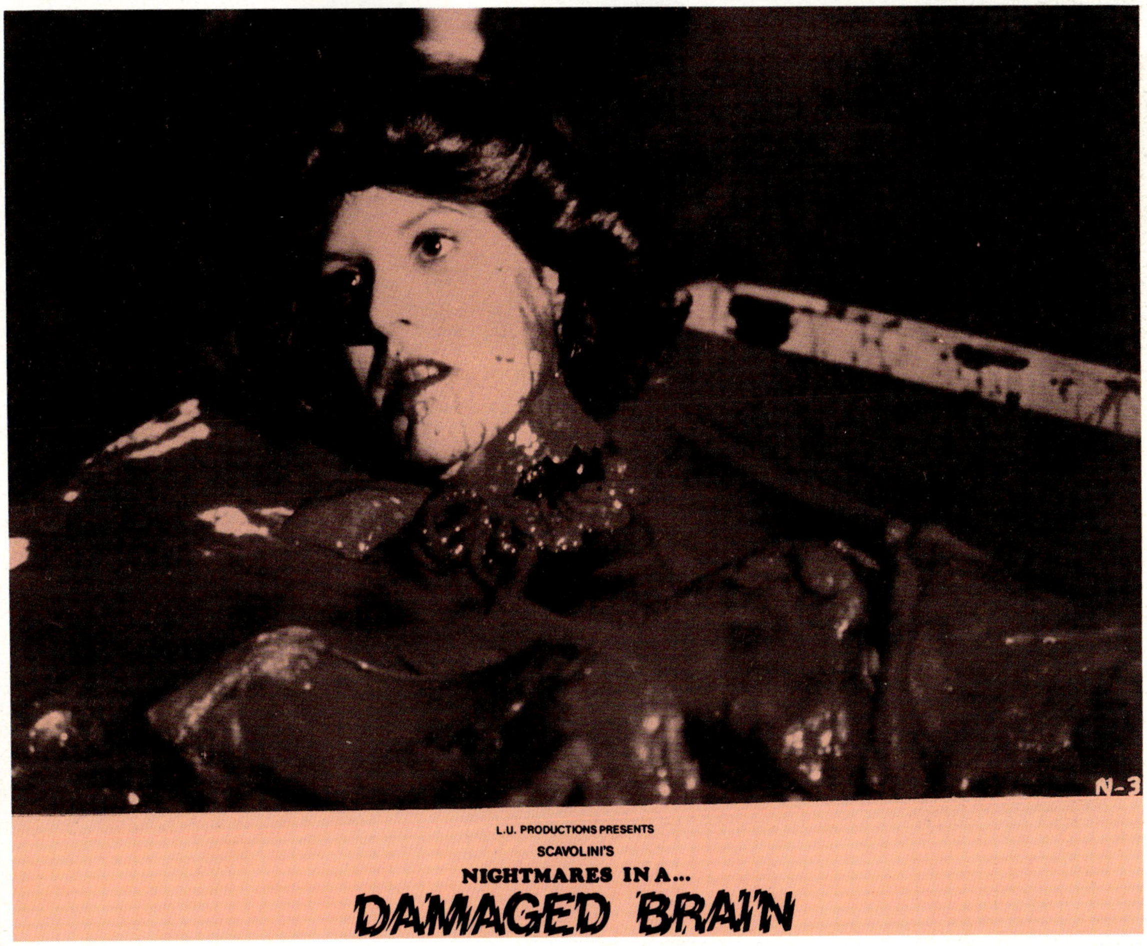

Above ***Nightmares In A Damaged Brain*** *(1982). There were many filmgoers who thought the damaged brain belonged to director Romano Scavolini. One of the violent and visceral shock-movies dubbed in Britain "video nasties".*

they should be swept out of sight.

This book isn't the place for a fully-fledged discussion on censorship, and my own views on the subject are already recorded in *The Video Nasties* (1984, Pluto Press). But it *is* the place for a brief account of these films and their putative appeal, and also their place in the horror genre.

First, let's point out that the movies are *so* diverse in their settings and storylines – from voodoo shenanigans in the subtropics (**Zombie Flesh-Eaters**, 1979) to rape and vengeance in America (**I Spit on Your Grave**, 1978) to monsters of the Id in Eastern Europe (**Possession**, 1981) – that their only common factor *is* their depiction of graphic violence. They do not constitute a genre or sub-genre in their own right, merely a new kind of audience-appeal phenomenon.

These are horror films in which, as hinted in Chapter 1, horrors must not only be done, they must be seen to be done. In **Zombie Flesh-Eaters**, a close-up shot depicts a wooden splinter slowly impaling a human eye. In **Cannibal Holocaust** (1979), mutilations, impalements and dismemberments happen under the unswerving eye of the camera (simulated, of course, but scarcely less vivid for that). In **Driller Killer** (1979), an electric drill pierces a human head. In **The Last House on the Left** (1972), a man's hand plunges into a living girl's chest and rips out her heart. In **Cannibal Terror** a live human is laid on a table where he

Below *More mayhem and dismemberment from* ***Zombie Flesh-Eaters*** *(1979). The use of primitive implements is a feature of the "video nasties" – never use a sophisticated weapon (like a gun) when you can hack, saw or impale.*

Right *Has this man thought of using a skin cream? Probably not, since he is one of the mutilation-prone zombies in* ***Dawn of the Dead*** *(George A. Romero, 1979).*

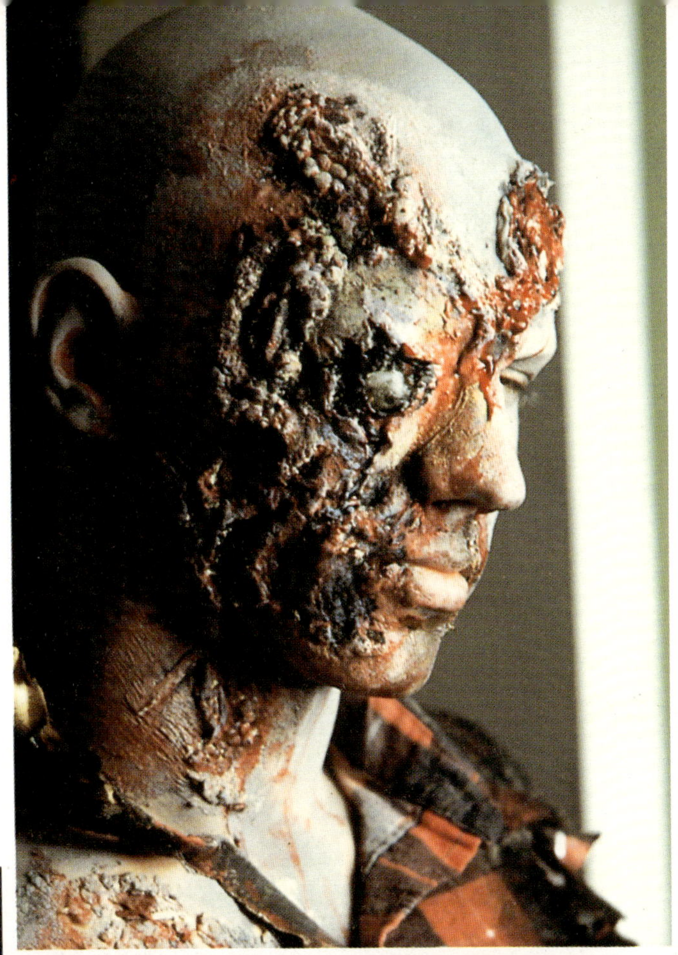

first has his left arm chopped off and then his stomach ripped open and his innards plucked out.

Confronting reality

There's no doubt that these movies are intended to appeal to the sadistic in us, or else to offer the cinematic equivalent of a quick finger down the throat. But whether you're titillated or nauseated by the "nasties", the one slender virtue one *can* ascribe to them is that they face us with the logical, unevasive reality of the emotional extremism we seek in horror films. They do not "tease" us with mysterious and unseen horror. They present horror to us on a slab; a butcher's slab. They are the logical product of the age of hi-fi media reportage. They are fictionalized versions of the unsparing horrors we saw in television reports from Vietnam, or even of the unsparing visceral truths which we confront every time we watch a surgical operation on a television program.

Above *Special effects had a field-day in John Carpenter's* ***The Thing*** *(1982), where very ugly things happen in a Polar research base. This is one of them.*

I believe that one of the reasons that the world's "moral majority" – from Britain's Festival of Light to America's Leagues of Decency – condemns such films, without ever having been known to condemn traditional or "classic" horror films, is similar to the reason they condemn sexual pornography. They believe that both sex and horror are acceptable when veiled by "mystery" and dignified by "romance". So the baroquely evasive eroticism of a Dietrich film or the sublimated passions of a Mills and Boon-type movie like **Love Story** (1970) are acceptable where the front-on couplings of a hardcore porno film are not. And in the same way the Gothically "evasive" horror of **Nosferatu** or **Frankenstein** – where violence is mist-wrapped, rhetorical or poetic, never visceral – is acceptable where the front-on horror of death, mutilation or pain is not.

This brings us to what has always seemed to me one of the great canards of movie criticism: that in depicting horror the "unseen" is somehow superior – more tasteful, more poetic, more powerful – to the seen. Of course, as soon as you start applying this rule to other arts, you realise how questionable it is. Sophocles, Euripides, Shakespeare, Goya, are but a few of the artists who when they wished to rub people's faces in a horrific event – the blinding of Gloucester, Saturn eating his children – would do so, and do so unforgettably. If the artist's imagination can outrun yours, there is no expressive gain in leaving a horrific event to *your* imagination. Only if the artist's imagination – and in cinema his special effects capability – do *not* match your powers of fantasy, does the principle of the power of the unseen necessarily hold good. One great service the "video nasties" have performed for us is to bring this question more into the open. In the current age of special effects virtuosity – when you can graphically simulate everything from a disembowelment to a man turning into a wolf – there is no guarantee at all that the film-maker's celluloid vision will be less powerful or vivid than your mental vision. So what price, dramatically at least, the "unseen"?

The poetry in horror

Yet though we must be wary of the invocation of "mystery" and "romance" when it is merely used by moral crusaders as a means to help bowdlerize blood-bolstered films, we cannot fling those qualities out of the horror genre altogether. For they *can* be a source of poetry and resonance. And more importantly, mystery and romance are strong enough qualities to flourish unscathed in many horror films that nobody would consider demurely inexplicit. The poetic *can* lie down with the bloodcurdling.

Right *A blue and green ghoulie from* ***Mausoleum*** *(1981), showing the tendency of monsters, when they have run out of on-screen victims, to reach out of the screen and go for the audience.*

Four examples. Hitchcock's **Psycho** (1960), vilified by many critics in its time as a piece of unworthy catchpenny sensationalism from a director who should know better, survives today – complete with stabbings, schizophrenia and mummified corpses – as an immeasurably rich and mysterious film. The "shocking" violence does not detract from that mystery, because the mystery is nothing to do with whether or not the scenes of horror are withheld from us. It's to do with character, guilt, forms of "forbidden" love – Norman Bates for his mother, Marion Crane (Janet Leigh) heading for her guilty love tryst with Sam Loomis (John Gavin) – and the way one macabre meeting-place helps to knot together several different destinies.

Similarly, Michael Powell's **Peeping Tom** (1959). When this British tale of a young photographer (Karl Boehm) who goes about murdering girls with the sharpened third leg of his tripod first came out, most English critics said it should go right back in again. One even urged that it be flushed down the nearest sewer. Yet, like **Psycho**, the movie is still with us and no new book on British horror ever fails to pick it out as a landmark. Again, the "mystery" is not in any gratuitous withholding of horror (for in a film about a mass-murderer there is surely such a thing as "gratuitous non-violence" rather than gratuitous violence, if the director may be deemed to have been exaggeratedly coy, inexplicit and evasive). The mystery is rather in the challenge given us to reconcile the hero's sweetly gentle manner with his hideous private actions. And the "romance" is in the hero's attempt to recapture the lost love and happiness of his childhood – before a brutalizing father (played by Powell himself) warped his growing-up – and thereby perhaps spring the catch on his own emotional prison.

Thirdly, Georges Franju's **Les Yeux Sans Visage** (**Eyes Without a Face**, 1959). This has several scenes designed to curdle your stomach, chiefly a facial "vivisection" performed by Pierre Brasseur's doctor on the lovely Edith Scob. As Mad Doctor movies go, this probably goes further than any. But it also has a surreal and eerie lyricism – in the black and white photography

Right *The eyes have it – hallucinatory peepers stare out at us from Brian De Palma's paranormal thriller* ***The Fury*** *(1978).*

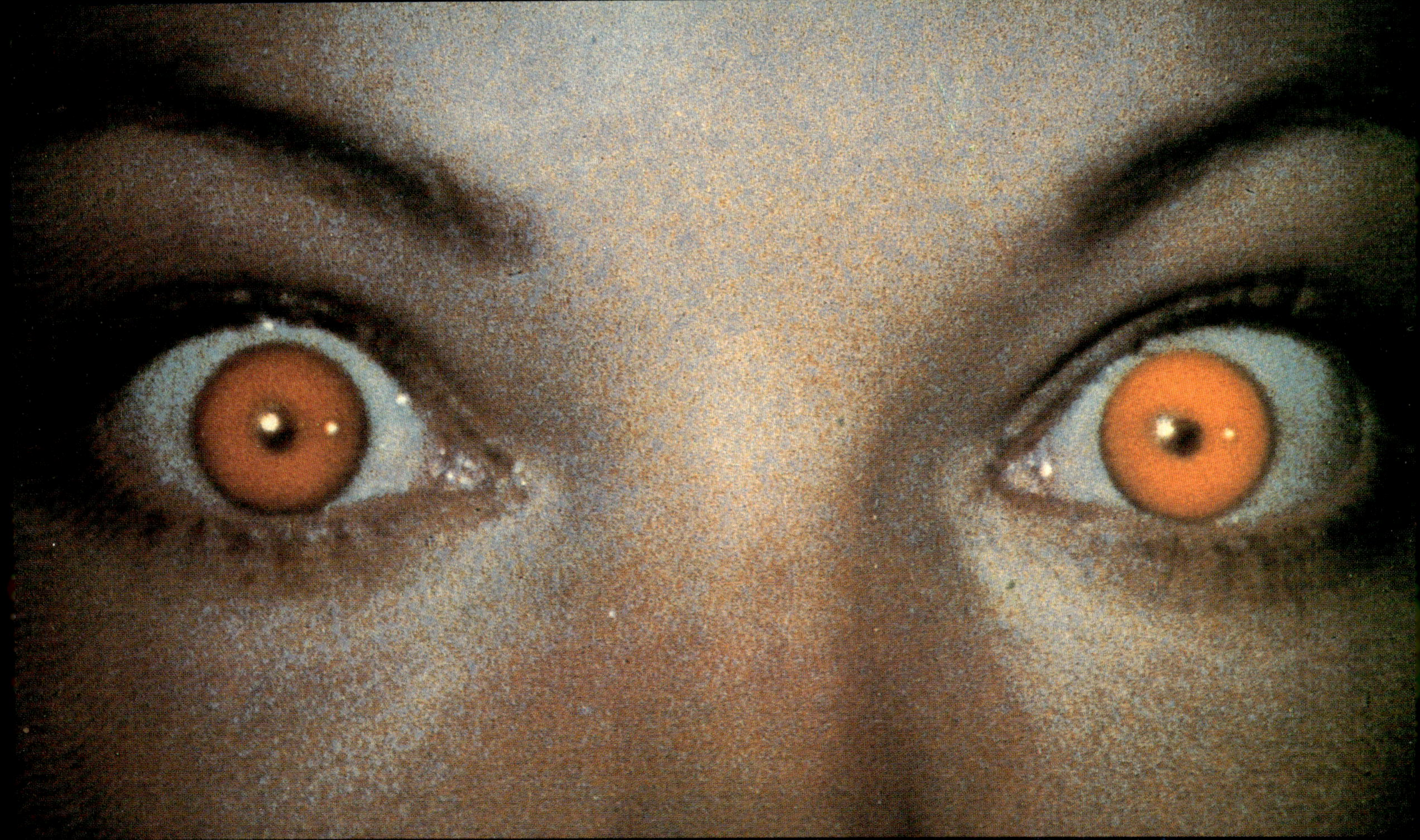

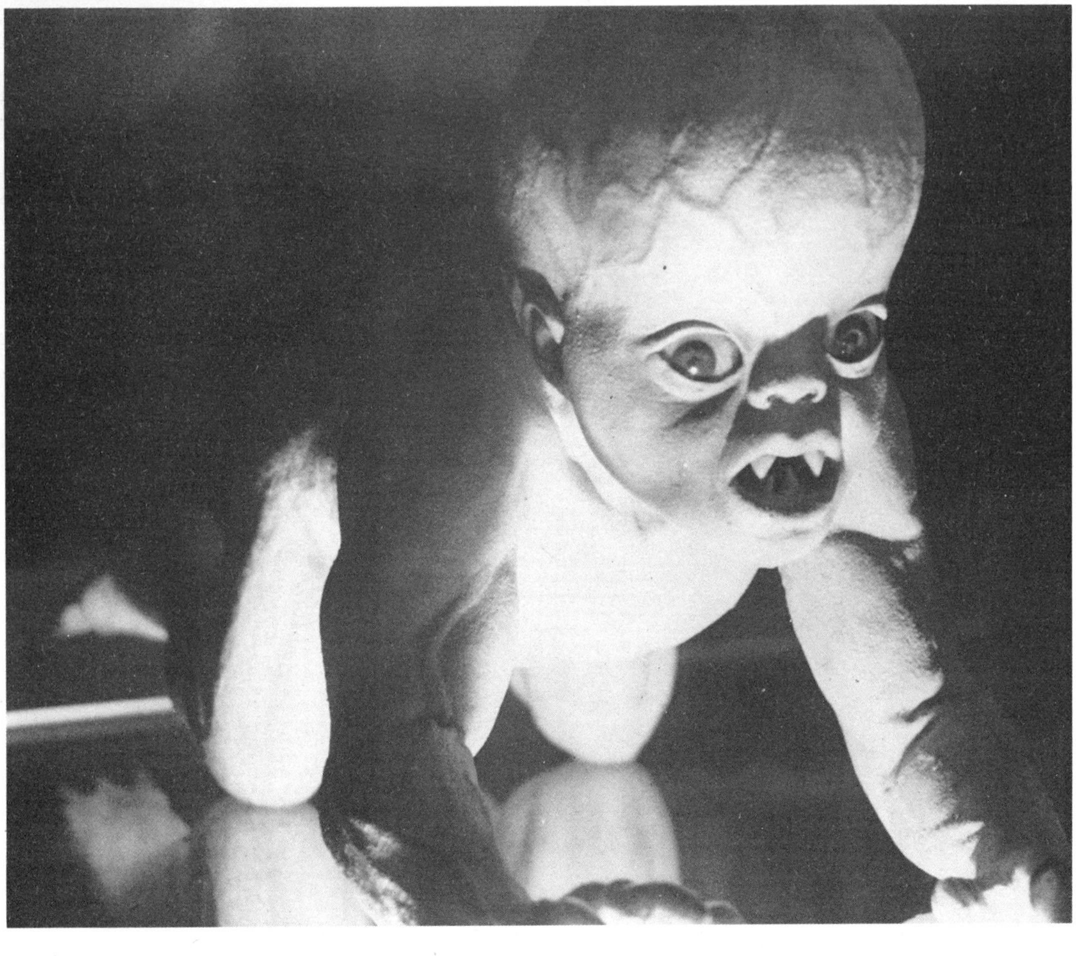

Above *A mutant baby was the scene-stealer – and scream-stealer – in David Lynch's* ***Eraserhead*** *(1976). Lynch stayed with deformity for his next film,* ***The Elephant Man****, made in 1980.*

Left *You wouldn't like to meet this baby in a darkened nursery either. The mad and murdering tot from* ***It's Alive*** *(1974).*

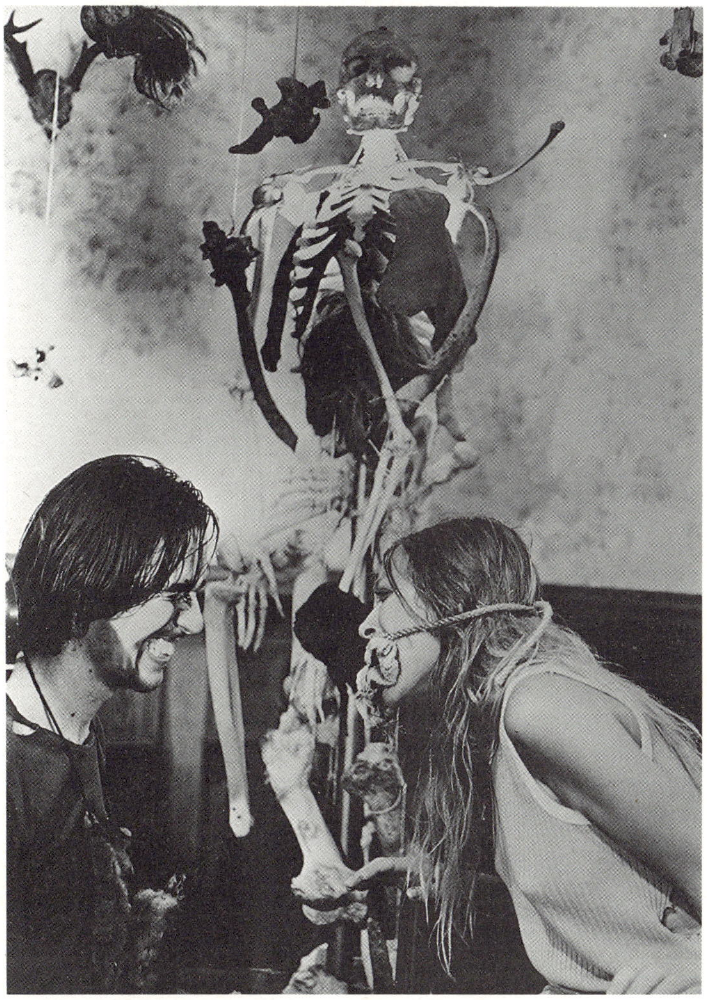

Left *Tobe Hooper's* ***The Texas Chainsaw Massacre*** *(1975). Edwin Neal and Marilyn Burns are, respectively, tormentor and victim in this blood-splattered shocker.*

Below *"Will somebody please help me?" But there was no help for* ***Psycho II*** *(1983), a doomed and catchpenny attempt to repeat the magic of Hitchcock's 1960 classic.*

(by German veteran Eugene Schüfftan), the sinuous moving camera and somnambulant, trance-like performances – that bring the film closer to Cocteau than to carnage cocktails like **Driller Killer**, **Cannibal Terror** or **The Texas Chainsaw Massacre.**

Franju is here exploring a parallel twilight world to that between life and death: the world between what makes us "human" and what makes us "inhuman". Is the heroine still "human" after having her features so macabrely remolded? Or is it the doctor whose humanity we should question after initiating this hideous surgery? (This is the conundrum of the concentration camps. Who was *truly* rendered subhuman by the horrors of Auschwitz or Dachau – the tortured or the torturers?)

Fourthly, Brian De Palma's **Body Double** (1984). This Chinese-box thriller of sex, murder and voyeurism was made by the director of **Carrie** (1976) and **Dressed to Kill** (1980), as a deliberately "outrageous" personal contribution to the video nasty style of exploitation film. Except, of course, that with De Palma a video nasty becomes a *thinking* man's video nasty. There is nudity, there is violence (a masked murderer, a driller killing), there are even scenes set on and around a porno film set. But, right from the start, the movie does a vertical take-off from the mire of meretriciousness into the ether of mystery. The ever-twining camera, the metallically gleaming colors, the astonishing sets (including a glassed and shimmering hilltop house like a space station) give the film a constant *trompe l'oeil* scintillation. And thematically its virtue is that it is as much *about* the Satanic mills of violence and sexuality as it is a product of them. Its subject is the voyeur in all of us: that evil, lynx-eyed Id compounded of the curious and covetous that can follow its prey as circuitously but single-mindedly as De Palma's ever-tracking camera.

Hidden horrors

But we shouldn't forget that, as well as "letting it all hang out" *vis-à-vis* the sensational, the post-1960s horror cinema can and often does keep it tantalizingly buttoned up. Two works that play brilliantly on the now-you-see-it-now-you-don't elusiveness of horror are Nicolas Roeg's **Don't Look Now** (1973) and George Miller's "Terror at 30,000 Feet" episode from **Twilight Zone: The Movie** (1983). The first maroons English couple Donald Sutherland and Julie Christie in that most hallucinatory of cities, Venice, and watches as the couple – she more than he – become obsessed

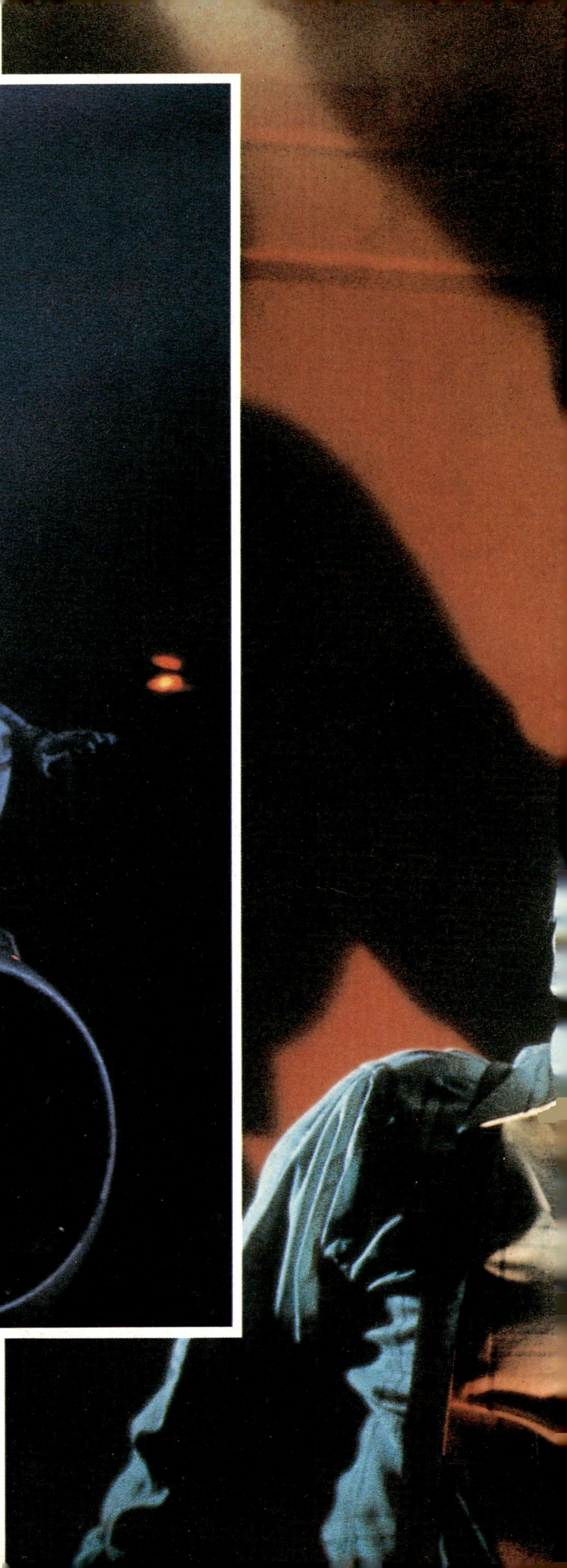

Twilight Zone: The Movie *(1983) tried to give a big-screen rush of blood to the old TV series – and mostly succeeded.* **Right** *Kevin McCarthy meets a giant bunny in one tale and in another* **(above)** *a "thing" sabotages a storm-tossed airplane.*

Above *William Katt has a blood-streaked prom night in Brian De Palma's* ***Carrie*** *(1976), based on Stephen King's supernatural novel.*

Above right *Another King novel was fed to the hungry histrionics of Jack Nicholson in* ***The Shining*** *(Stanley Kubrick, 1980).*

Right *The car of your dreams... or your nightmares? Stephen King rides again in this tale of a demonic Plymouth called* ***Christine*** *(1983), based on King's novel of the same name.*

with the idea that their lately drowned daughter's spirit is alive and well and near them. Though not a "horror film", **Don't Look Now** sustains a nonstop mood of fear and apprehension and ends in a grisly *éclat* of true terror featuring a red dwarf, a sharp knife and a slashed throat.

The **Twilight Zone** episode directed by George (**Mad Max**) Miller is a little *tour de force*. It's a story of suggestibility spiralling into stark terror. John Lithgow is the nervous air passenger flying through a thunderstorm, who's convinced he sees a "thing" far out on the wing dismantling one of the plane's engines. But only during lightning bolts is it visible and, since the stewardesses have already marked him down as a hysteric, no one on the plane will believe him. The more fools they, of course, because the "thing" exists. And at the movie's thunderclap high-point it scuttles right up to Lithgow's window and scares the living daylights out of him (and us) with its hideous grinning face, like a flayed gargoyle.

This kind of playful, prankster horror tale – in which the portrayal of gathering terror in the victim is more important than any detailed portrait of his tormenter – is also typical of Stephen King's horror stories. King has turned the penning of horror tales into a whole cottage, or carnage, industry. And Hollywood has seized almost every novel he's written to turn it into celluloid: **Carrie** (1976), **The Shining** (1980), **Christine** (1983), **Cujo** (1983), **The Dead Zone** (1983) and **Firestarter** (1984). In addition, King wrote an original screenplay, **Creepshow** – his least effective film – which George (**Night of the Living Dead**) Romero directed in 1982.

Though the characters and settings may differ, the basic ingredients of a King story don't. They're all about supernatural gifts and/or spiritual possession. In

Above *"Horror" styles and special effects meet the comedy market. Dan Aykroyd and Bill Murray lead the spook-fighters in the 1984 box-office hit* ***Ghostbusters.***

Carrie, a girl discovers she has telekinetic gifts and uses them in a *walpurgisnacht* of revenge on her prank-playing schoolmates. In **The Shining**, evil spirits in a snowbound off-season Colorado hotel gradually "take over" the hotel's caretaker and terrorize his family. **Christine** is about a demon-possessed car, **Cujo** about a similarly possessed dog. And in **Dead Zone** and **Firestarter** we have, as hero and heroine respectively, a man who can foretell the future and a little girl who can start fires with her mind.

States of mind

The King movies, by and large, are far less bloodcurdling than the King novels. And the fact that they've been directed by less and less distinguished directors as the series runs on (from De Palma and Kubrick to Lewis Teague and Mark Lester) suggests the movie industry is twigging to this – or realizes that there's a special kind of spookiness in King's writing that doesn't translate to the screen. Only **Carrie**, directed by Brian De Palma with demonic *élan*, kaleidoscopic visuals and a superpowered Sissy Spacek, works at white heat throughout. And though one admires Kubrick's **The Shining** (1980) for its metaphysics and mazy obsessionalism – here are Jack Nicholson, Shelley Duvall and Danny Lloyd endlessly chasing each other's psyches in an inner circle of their homemade Hell – it seldom harrows or terrifies.

What's "untranslatable" in King's novels is the fact that they're about states of mind rather than objectified demons or devils, ghosts or ghouls. A sense of prickly fear and irrational panic is built up so vividly in the narrative, and in the rhythms of King's jagged, precipitate prose – like a man talking too fast to conceal his terror – that "ordinary" objects or creatures, like a car or a dog, can be catalyzed into the extraordinary without any help from galumphing visual details. But in cinema the "eye" is God, and states of mind are useless unless they can be turned into visual images. And all too often they can't. In John Carpenter's **Christine** the car – for all its sinisterly blazing headlights and metamorphosing metalwork – remains a car. In Lewis Teague's **Cujo** the dog remains a dog, for all its megadecibel barking and its frantically applied streaks of bile, blood and saliva.

Yet there's a thread running through King's tales that can guide us towards the heart of the modern horror labyrinth both in fiction and on film. The old polarity between personified Good and Evil that characterized the "classic" horror films – a hero or heroine at bay against a lumbering monster (Frankenstein) or a Machiavellian demon (Dracula) – has yielded to a line in horror protagonists who contain *within themselves* the forces of good and evil. Hence the prominence since the 1960s of films about possession (**Exorcists**, **Omens**, **Amityvilles**), of tales of mutant and schizophrenic horror figures like the werewolf, and of Stephen King's own brand of supernatural yarn where the initially innocent central character is "taken over" by good or bad spiritual forces.

And even the movies that *seem* to be about Us (hero or heroine) versus Them (ogres or occupiers) are increasingly ambivalent. The horrific acts of violence in the **Friday the 13th** series are seldom visited on the entirely innocent. The frequency with which sex acts take place, for example, just before the young participants are impaled or decapitated suggests that there's a Hollywood puritanism at work here: that the murdered girls and youths are not just hapless victims of Fate but adventurers into guilt who somehow invite their own doom.

Likewise in the "video nasties" the division between Good and Bad, Innocence and Corruption, is increasingly blurred. The raped heroine of **I Spit On Your Grave** becomes as savage and brutal as her assailants when she takes up the quest for vengeance. In **Nightmares in a Damaged Brain** (1981), an "innocent" child, traumatized by the sight of his father making love, becomes a deranged killer. And in **Cannibal Holocaust** the man-eating savages of a South American jungle visit their horrors not on a group of innocents lost in the wilderness but on a prurient, ruthless and almost equally brutal group of documentary film-makers (!), one of whose favorite pastimes is to burn down native villages and film the inhabitants going up in flames with their dwellings.

Return of the werewolf

The most visually effective embodiment of this ambivalence in the modern horror cinema is the werewolf. He has become the era's most "magnetic" movie myth, drawing to the lodestone of his multiple nature

Below *Why go out for the evening when you can be struck by lightning in your own room? A nasty moment for a young girl in* ***The Entity*** *(1981), one of the paranormal pics popular in the late 1970s/early 1980s.*

features of innocence and evil alike; of Dracula's subtle guile and Frankenstein's brute instinct, of the metamorphosed and the monstrous, the "human" and the inhuman. He is the consummation of the post-1960s horror creed that Evil is not outside us, it is in us: the enemy cannot be glibly totemized as the Other, for we will find him easily enough in ourselves.

The werewolf is also, of course, today's greatest walking advertisement for state-of-the-art special effects in the horror film. The lupine metamorphoses devised by Rob Bottin for **The Howling** and Rick Baker for **An American Werewolf In London** (both 1981) boggled the mind – human faces creaking and stretching into prognathous jaws, fingers cracking into hairy claws, feet bursting their shoes to thrust out bony paws – and these mutations have thrilled audiences again in **The Company of Wolves** (1984).

The last-named film is the most potent and poetic contribution to the New Werewolfery so far. If **The Howling** and **An American Werewolf** were glorified japes, wringing campy, modernist variations from the age-old carcass of the body lycanthropic, first **Wolfen** (1981) and then **The Company of Wolves** showed that there could be more to this sub-genre than a mere fleeting giggle and spine-tingle.

In **Wolfen**, directed by Mike Wadleigh of **Woodstock**, suggesting he had decided the time had come to swap flower power for feral power, the werewolf leaps up at our throats as if out of the American past itself. Stratified with history – the locations include a former Red Indian hunting ground and a memorial windmill commemorating New York's first Dutch settlers – the movie suggests that our past is so silted up with a compound of good and evil, corruption and innocence, that none of us can *ever* claim to be entirely one or the other. The werewolf is therefore our heraldic animal; condemned to prowl the earth forever, mutating at the moon's whim, a haunted hybrid of man and beast, the divine and the debased.

In **The Company of Wolves**, directed by Neil Jordan from a screenplay by novelist Angela Carter, this helpless mutability creates a rich tragic-erotic fable. Ringing Freudian changes on the Red Riding Hood story, it leaves us in no doubt of the wolf's symbolic role as a sexual Id. There's even a grim parody of canine tumescence in the transformation scenes, as the red and throbbing wolf-heads push out from the human faces in which they're sheathed. But as well as being a Freudian fantasia on a fairytale theme, the film

Left *The penalty for failing to keep the wolf from the door. A victim succumbs to lycanthropy as the cinema's werewolf fashion romps on.* ***The Howling*** *(1981).*

Above and left *Two of the wolfish transformations brilliantly conceived by make-up ace Rick Baker for* ***An American Werewolf in London*** *(1981). John Landis directed cleverly for an excellent mixture of terror and tongue-in-cheek.*

Above ***The Company of Wolves*** *(1984). Director Neil Jordan co-wrote the script with fantasy novelist Angela Carter – and together they fashioned a memorable horror fable, part feral, part Freudian.*

is of mighty importance to the horror genre because it shows that the mythic and transfigurative side of movie art can still thrive even in an age of post-**Texas Chainsaw** bloodlust.

And it also proves that the imagery of horror in the cinema depends more than that of any other genre on a constant inspirational shuttle service between Past and Present. The most powerful horror icons may well be the oldest we have, reinterpreted anew for each new generation. And just as the werewolf has been brought out of mothballs in recent times for spring-cleaning and renovation – and he goes back at least fifty years, to Stuart Walker's **The Werewolf of London** (1935) – so an age may come when a more polarized or Manichean vision of good and evil, and a more dualistic vision of evil itself, will restore, changed but still recognizable, our old friends Frankenstein and Dracula. In horror films, as in human nature, there is nothing new under the moon.

TITLE CHANGES

U.S. title	**U.K. title**
Abbott and Costello Meet Frankenstein (1948)	Abbott and Costello Meet the Ghosts
Attack of the Mushroom People (1963)	Matango – Fungus of Terror
The Black Cat (1934)	The House of Doom
Horror of Dracula (1958)	Dracula
House of Usher (1960)	The Fall of the House of Usher
The Most Dangerous Game (1932)	The Hounds of Zaroff
The She Beast (1965)	The Revenge of the Blood Beast

PICTURE CREDITS

Ronald Grant 14, 15 bottom, 23, 28, 29 top, 33 top, 35 bottom, 44, 55, 59 middle, 60-61, 63 bottom, 80, 84 top **Alan Jones** 78-79 **Kobal Collection** title, 9, 13, 15 top, 19 top, 24-26, 27 top, 29 bottom, 31, 36, 39, 40, 41 bottom, 42, 46, 47, 50-54, 56-57, 59 top, 59 bottom, 65, 72 top, 73, 75, 81 bottom, 85 left, 86-87, 88 **Alan McKenzie** half title, 6-7, 8, 10-12, 16, 17 top, 19 bottom, 20-22, 27 bottom, 30, 32, 33 bottom, 34, 35 top, 37 top, 38, 41 top, 43, 45, 48, 49, 57-58, 60, 62, 63 top, 64, 66-67, 71 bottom, 74, 81 top, 83, 84 bottom, 86, 90-93, 94 top, 95 endpapers **Rex Features** contents, 17 bottom, 18, 37 bottom, 66, 68-69, 71 top, 71 inset, 72 bottom, 76-77, 85 right, 89

Front cover: **Alan McKenzie** background, bottom right **Kobal Collection** bottom left and middle.

Back cover: **Alan McKenzie**

Many of the illustrations come from stills issued to publicize films or distributed by the following companies:– AIP/Alta Vista, Alpha Films, Colombia/Sabre, Hammer Film Productions, MGM, Miracle Films, Neptun-Film, Paramount, Pressman Williams, RKO, Seda Spettacoli, Simon, TCF/Frank Yablins, Twentieth Century Fox, Universal Pictures, Warner, Paul Wegner.